Pull Thinking®

Harness the Power of Pull to Fuel Growth, and Ignite Performance
by
Aligning People, Culture and Purpose

Volume I

ISBN 0-9726403-0-4 (Volume I)

Printed in the United States of America

14   13   12   11   10   9   8

Pull Thinking ®

Harness the Power of Pull to Fuel Growth, and Ignite Performance
by
Aligning People, Culture and Purpose

Volume I

Kenneth E. Meyer

with
Jeffrey A. Lebow

Page	Contents
v	Preface
1	Introduction
18	Step 1 — The Pull Principle®
40	Step 2 — Thinking Pull
68	Step 3 — The First Pull Question Purpose Creates Structure
106	Step 4 — The Second Pull Question Define Measures of Success
156	Step 5 — The Third Pull Question Establish Actual Measurements
202	Step 6 — The Fourth Pull Question Determine the Frequency of Each Measurement
240	Step 7 — Harness the Power of Pull Measure, Acknowledge, Take Action, Solve Problems
280	Step 8 — Ultimate Service — What's Next?
289	*Appendix A — Measurement Form*
291	*Appendix B — Frequently Asked Questions*
294	*Appendix C — Glossary*
301	*Appendix D — Resources*
310	*Acknowledgements*
311	*About the Author*

PREFACE

You seem to be doing all the right things. You are current with what all the latest business book authors are saying and apply (as best you can) what those thought leaders and business gurus are saying. You are even among the very small percent that become a model of success being written about by one of those major authors. Yet, you find that you still have internal conflicts and communication issues between people and teams causing tense relationships and other difficulties. You can't understand why this is happening. Why isn't <u>everyone</u> cooperating and happy? What's missing?

You have tried to apply what you read in the latest business book, but nothing seems to stick. It seems so easy when you read those case study examples of very successful companies like GE or Bank of America or EDS. You keep buying those books as they appear in hopes of finding the right solution that will ignite your employees and turn your business around.

The question that needs to be asked is: How do your internal and external customers want your business to be organized, to operate, to handle financial flow, etc. Like the snow flake, there is only one particular way that will produce the utmost best, most efficient process that creates the product and service experiences that your end customer wants. There is no one common formula for all of us to follow. The reality of it is that it is an individual thing. You need to figure out what is best for you.

Many successful businesses are led by CEO's, mentored by other successful leaders and or students of various business authors, achieve ultimate successful application of what they learned to their own businesses. Their successes are then chronicled in the latest business success book. Thus providing a platform on which the next business leaders build their success. And so we go.

Business authors today certainly provide great insight and advice from the stand point of synthesizing what works for one business leader or another. Authors attempt to discover how successful business leaders think and often suggest copying their habits as a way to become as successful. One author tells us to do what we are best at and pick people to do what they are best at. Another shows us what measurements successful companies have in common.

Another says that it's about having a leader that knows how to execute.

They are all heading in the right direction, and incremental improvements are certainly accomplished by some. The problem is, they leave out how to connect people to work together for the customer's benefit. All of them are high level and do not really talk to all levels of an organization.

What's different? Three examples:

Curt Coffman and Gabriel Gonzalez-Molina, Ph.D. in *Follow This Path*, recommend emotional engagement as one of the keys to understanding successful business leaders today. "The accepted conclusions about emotions indicate that they are objective, measurable, and universal to all human feelings. The implications of the effects of emotions as they relate to the workplace and to customer behavior are simple but powerful." … "But emotions are the mechanisms of our mind least understood by management – hence the great opportunity for organizations." … "As opposed to a more transactional approach to leadership, an approach in which leaders prescribe for employees what to do, transformational leadership involves leaders broadening and elevating the interests of their employees. This can be accomplished by creating awareness and acceptance of the purposes and mission of the organization and looking beyond self-interest to the interest of the group as a whole." [1] They go on and provide the measures the leaders use to create this awareness in an organization. The difference that Pull Thinking brings is to tie the measurements to purposes in a structured way within the flow of customer service. Pull Thinking provides an excellent context for the very important measurements that the Gallup organization presents.

Jim Collins in *Good to Great* has the Three Circles of the Hedgehog Concept[2] as the cornerstone of the book: 1) What you are

---

[1] Coffman, Curt and Gonzalez-Molina, Gabriel, *Follow This Path*, Warner Books, Inc, 2002 pages 235, 236

[2] Collins, Jim, *Good to Great*, HarperCollins Puplishers, 2001, page 96

deeply passionate about; 2) What you can be the best in the world at; and 3) What drives your economic engine. Using this at a high level certainly brought results to the companies chronicled in the book, but this does not work to bring buy in and alignment to all levels of an organization. It does not show individuals up and down the line how to connect to the organizational structure, how to become customer focused, or how to be empowered to solve their own problems. It does not build teams or change mindsets. <u>With Pull Thinking, the three Hedgehog Concept circles are addressed automatically.</u> <u>Pull Thinking ensures an internal/external customer focus and knowledge of how to structure the environment in support of the internal and external customers of the whole organization.</u> You will see how those three circles represent purposes – each having a connection in the service flow structure discussed in Step 3. The three circles are really Measures of Success when seen from a Pull Thinking context (Step 1). You will learn why this is only one of the Four Dimensions of Alignment. Purpose, Measurement and Frequency of Measurement also need to be addressed. The three circles also represent choices every company needs to make at all levels. The most important aspect to note is what is missing: <u>the customer</u>, both internal (employees) and external.

Larry Bossidy and Ram Charan in *Execution – The Discipline of Getting Things Done*, say: "In its most fundamental sense, execution is a systematic way of exposing reality and acting on it. Most companies don't face reality very well…that's the basic reason they can't execute." … "Execution is the job of the business leader." … "There's a saying we recently heard: We don't think ourselves into a new way of acting, we act ourselves into a new way of thinking. Acting your way into a new way of thinking begins with demystifying the word *culture*…Stripped to its essentials; an organization's culture is the sum of its shared values, beliefs, and norms of behavior." … "If a company rewards and promotes people for execution, its culture will change." [3] Conversely this approach will not produce maximum results because the mindset has not been

---

[3] Bossidy, Larry and Charan, Ram, *Execution – The Discipline of Getting Things Done*, Crown Business publisher, 2002, pages 22, 89 and 92

addressed. For that to happen, the theoretical basis for understanding how best to change needs to change. <u>The difference is that Pull Thinking provides a practical organizational alignment strategy based on profound simple ancient truth. In present day language it allows you to make sense out of difficult problems.</u> The most efficient way to execute is to think your way into acting. Thinking comes first – actions follow. To execute first and think second is simply more difficult and more costly and the results are less than what is possible.

The culture difference:

We are talking about culture and the fundamental building blocks of business – PEOPLE and how people think – their mindsets. These authors do address behavior and motivation issues. But they fail to recognize that when thinking is addressed first these issues become less difficult. The questions answered in this book are: How do you provide a culture that supports the best service possible for any business? How do you ensure profitable growth year after year? And: How do you get Four Dimensional Alignment^{SM} throughout the organization?

Many of the best-run businesses have goals and structures in place at all levels and appear to be doing all the right things as read in the latest business books. Yet communications problems, tense relationships and low morale still exist. What's different about Pull Thinking is that it shows first why this is happening; and, second, shows everyone at all levels what to do about it.

Pull Thinking is about a practical way for people to connect with each other and to ultimately connect with the internal/external customers and suppliers with a focus on purpose and service. As a result, it <u>creates customer-focused listening and strategic alignment</u> at all levels beginning at the individual level. Because of this connectedness, there is buy-in that will make your business processes and your customers' business processes more successful and sustainable. How? By addressing how we think as individuals, as teams, as organizations, as integral parts of the communities in which we serve, and how to organize to always be efficiently responsive to their changing needs.

The value difference:

With Pull Thinking three levels of value result: 1.) the individual people that make up companies; 2.) the company's processes and strategies that support the individuals providing services to external customers; and, as a result: 3.) the company's customers. Pull Thinking provides a Service Flow Pull Structure that connects the whole service supply chain. Jeff Thull in his article entitled *Winning Profitable Customers* said "It's no longer enough to offer a value-added product. You must leverage your value all the way through to your customers' customers…we are living and working in a time called the 'third era' of professional selling – but too many sales organizations are still operating in an outdated mindset." In his synopsis, he refers to this as when your services go beyond the first level: a good price; beyond the second level: helping your customers' processes; and into the third level: your customers' customers benefit from your products and services. He said that this third level of sales professional is when: "You have become an integral part of their business, a source of competitive advantage, you're making their life easier, and you're contributing to their measurable success."[4]

The bottom line:

When you make Pull Thinking an integral part of your business, it becomes a source of competitive advantage. It makes life easier for your company and your customers thus contributing measurable success to both. You have fun!

---

[4] From an article by Jeff Thull called *Winning Profitable Customers*, Catalyst Magazine, June 2004, page 24

Why write this book?

Simple—when one discovers something new and important, it's natural to want to share the discovery. This is one of those discoveries.

Pull Thinking was a light bulb of discovery born out of my frustration with implementing change in organizations. The discovery was that the entire universe is one magnificent, elegant *Pull System!* Everything nature creates is created by *Pulling!* Every action is the result of a *Pull.* Can you think of any more perfect creative process than Mother Nature?

What if this is how nature thinks? What if Pull Thinking is mental ergonomics—the easiest way to think?

I needed to capture the light bulb discovery in a way that's easy to communicate and understand, so I framed it in what I call "The Pull Principle" and "Pull Thinking." Pull Thinking brings the Pull Principle to life and makes Pull real—something we can all measure, something we can all learn to create.

The next step was to put it to work in my life and career. As a result of Pull Thinking, my personal effectiveness increased enormously. Once I applied Pull Thinking, I could solve difficult problems very quickly. Even more important, it's been very effective for others—I found myself able to talk to CEOs, executives, supervisors, and shop floor workers in a way that had them listening differently. The language of Pull Thinking made it easy for them to open their minds to new ideas and discover solutions for themselves.

I found that we are all pulled and are pulling everyday. The word pull is already a big part of our common language as both a noun and a verb—"he has pull," or "pull a team together," or "pull your own weight." Sometimes we're aware of what is pulling, sometimes we're not.

What if we could learn to Pull all the time—could we be more on-target and purposeful?

We all know people who have "magnetic" personalities. What if being "magnetic" wasn't just something one is born with, and thus seemingly out of our control? What if it was something we could learn to use to create our own personal and business magnetism?

What if we could learn to *Harness the Power of Pull?*

Some of what you will read here may sound familiar. As time goes on, I see more and more evidence that people are beginning to understand the importance of understanding "Pull." For example, the new *Science of Chaos* has scientists rethinking their understanding of the universe and talk about the <u>elegant order underlying the apparent chaos</u> that is literally Pulling the creation of the universe.

In the 2005 Number 3 issue of the McKinsey quarterly, authors John Seely Brown and John Hagel in their paper called *"From push to pull: The next frontier of innovation*[5]*"* have chronicled how a few fringe companies in the world have found the value of pull systems over push systems. One of the key messages they write talks about how the discovery of the power and efficiency of pull systems will have corporate executives reassessing how they do business.

Another example: We've all been caught up in the push to create vision and mission statements to pull our organizations together. Many of us are left wondering why. These statements hang on walls across corporate America, but more often than not, nothing has changed in our day-to-day routine. Organizations across the country attempt to implement and sustain various improvement initiatives, such as balanced scorecard, six sigma, total quality, team development, cellular manufacturing and pull systems, to name just a few. The result? Most of us become frustrated and disillusioned because implementation has proven to be difficult or impossible.

Pull Thinking provides the context that gives luster, passion and power to those important statements and initiatives—and provides the tools to assure their sustained realization and harness unseen forces to align with our efforts drawing us towards our vision of success.

For me, the early application of Pull Thinking happened to be in manufacturing, but I could have been in any business. It began with a personal shift in thinking. The application is universal, because it's simply a different way of thinking first. Action comes second. But this is for you to discover. Then you can apply it in your own

---

[5] The McKinsey Quarterly, 2005 Number 3

situation. After many years of testing, I have yet to find any contradictions or incompatibilities. It simply always works.

Pull Thinking isn't the result of years of studying other thinkers and business case studies or collecting the best ideas and synthesizing them into one principle. The discovery of the Pull Principal and Pull Thinking came upon me in a flash. I spent the next several years discovering new validations and learning new applications. For me, it was like discovering fire and then figuring out how to harness its power to keep warm, cook food, forge steel, and launch rockets.

I've only begun to scratch the surface of the potential of *Pull Thinking*. I was "Pulled" to write this book so everyone could learn to "*Pull together.*"

Kenneth E. Meyer
ken@pullthinking.com
www.pullthinking.com
Atlanta, GA
Summer 2004

"Sailing out of Chaos..."

INTRODUCTION

The team on the sailboat has harnessed the power of Pull. Working together, they're sailing through the chaos of the storm into the calm seas and clarity of the sunlight. Each person shares the purpose of the team, knows his or her role in its achievement, and understands what individual success and success for the team looks like.

The captain of this vessel doesn't have to tell this team what to do and when to do it. Indeed, if he did, this vessel could be lost. He simply sets the direction, the individuals know which lines to pull to turn the sails and steer towards success.

This book is about a powerful distinction between Push and Pull. Contrary to popular belief, the most efficient way to sail is to be in the pull of the wind.[6] The same is true in business. Where people are pushed to do what needs to be done, the result is limited success.

When they are pulled toward a shared purpose and know how what they do really matters, they have integrity and a passion for improving performance. Everyone knows who they are serving and knows how to measure their own success and they get frequent candid feedback. This is an environment that people want to work in where turnover is very low and the internal/external customer/supplier service experience is excellent throughout the business enterprise.

What if there was a mentally ergonomic way to create that kind of team?

What if the context for creating and growing any business of any size lay in the forces of Pull and Push? Wouldn't there be power in being able to identify and understand these forces?

What if the process of applying this understanding enrolled everyone around you in realizing your vision and passion? Wouldn't that mean that you could start tomorrow?

Enter Pull Thinking

---

[6] Even when sailing upwind using a spinnaker, the fastest speeds are achieved by sailing several degrees off 180^0 to create an aerofoil from the Pull of the wind.

In Pull Thinking, there are three tools:

> 1. **The Pull Principle**®, three tenets define the Pull force and the distinction between Push and Pull.
> 2. **The Four Pull Questions**ˢᴹ, identify the actual Pull forces present and establish a measure on creating Ultimate Service.
> 3. **The Pull Structure**ˢᴹ, a methodology for identifying and creating the relationship between Pull forces necessary to enable the flow of Ultimate Service.

1. The Pull Principle

Here's where you begin the practical application of Pull Thinking. This principle is the driving force behind the entire methodology. And its power was described by Aristotle over a thousand years ago:

"A prime mover that moves everything without itself moving ... must cause motion by being attractive rather than propulsive" - *Aristotle, 350BC*

In other words, you use less energy and garner greater results when you attract or *Pull* people into what you need done, as opposed to when you *Push* them. Consider the truths about *Pull*:

The Pull Principle

- The primary force that causes all movement is a Pull force; a Push force is the result of (or a response to) a Pull force.
- The most efficient way to create, grow, and improve is to Pull.
- Pull is the creative force of nature that no one can avoid or alter.

Push is a force that creates a natural kind of reluctance or resistance. *Pull*, on the other hand, works as a kind of magnet. It's what people find compelling about what you're trying to do. It's the "what's in it for me" factor. And it also determines what's in it for everyone else.

2. The Four Pull Questions

1. What is the purpose?
2. What are the Measures of Success?
3. What is actually being measured?
4. What is the frequency with which the measurements are being taken?

Clear answers to all of the Four Pull Questions, mutually understood and agreed upon between supplier and customer, define a Pull force. Why four questions? The short answer is: because that's how many it takes to define a Pull. These seemingly simple questions are used to uncover problem areas and define accountabilities. Questions that help define purpose and measures of success. Questions that identify the Pull. All of which leads to Ultimate Service Flow and alignment—delivering optimal collaboration, efficiency and results. Together they form a link in the service flow supply chain discussed in detail in Step 3.

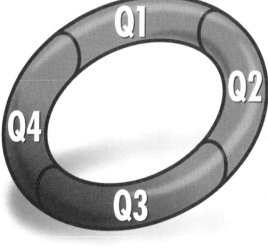

1. What is the purpose?

2. What are the measures of success?

4. What is the frequency with which the measurements are being taken?

3. What is actually being measured?

Examples of the Four Pull Questions:

Personal
1. What is the purpose? To reach my ideal weight.
2. What are the Measures of Success? *Losing 30 pounds in six months.*
3. What is actually being measured? *The number of pounds and the amount of time.*
4. How often are measurements being taken? *Weighing once a day.*

Sales
1. What is the purpose? *To increase sales.*
2. What are the Measures of Success? *Selling 20 more cars each month.*
3. What is actually being measured? *The number of cars sold and the amount of time.*
4. How often are measurements being taken? *Sales are reported weekly.*

Production

1. What is the purpose? *To increase the production and improve the quality of the product.*
2. What are the Measures of Success? *Producing 50 more TVs a month with no more than one defect per 1,000.*
3. What is actually being measured? *The number of TVs produced and the number of defects for every 1000 TVs.*
4. How often are measurements being taken? *There are __daily__ reports of TVs coming off the assembly lines and __hourly__ reports of the # of defects.*

Integrity matters—actions speak louder than words

The Four Pull Questions work together to ensure integrity. Questions 1 & 2 are what we say; Questions 3 & 4 are what we do.

If a customer (internal or external) does not tell you their Measures of Success, then a clear Pull may not be known until after a misstep during a trial and error process. If a customer says one thing but means another, then integrity of purpose is not established and a breakdown of service may be imminent. Actions need to be kept in balance with our words.

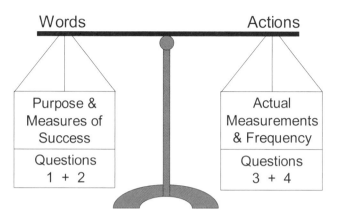

Communication is the thread that connects the supplier and customer, and asking the right questions ensures <u>alignment</u> to all Four Pull Questions. There is service with integrity. There is <u>Four Dimensional Alignment</u>.

Businesses measure and people have purposes, but often one is not connected to the other or is connected inappropriately. There are "pieces" of "Pull" floating around (Figure 1) needing to be assembled into defined Pulls (Figure 2), then put into a Pull structure (Figure 3). Once the structure is known, completing the "Pulls" by answering the questions becomes the strategy for improvement towards Ultimate Service Flow (Figure 4). Ultimate service should be the goal of every business. As you'll see, it's the key to personal and professional success.

Not having the answers to all four questions causes chaos with the service experience. The flow of service is impeded as depicted in Condition 2 on page 11. The completed Pull Structure acts like a laser; energy is focused on the most important problem. Problems are quickly solved. Priorities are easier to set.

Typically, monetary measurements on costs and profitability are prevalent. These measures are not connected to purpose; people are left to fill in their own purposes to serve. Often it comes down to serving a manager or supervisor instead of having a focus or connection with the internal or external customers needs. Is there any wonder why there are communication problems, complaints, or chaos? (Figure 1) It's a major reason why people hop from one organization to another in search of a better working environment.

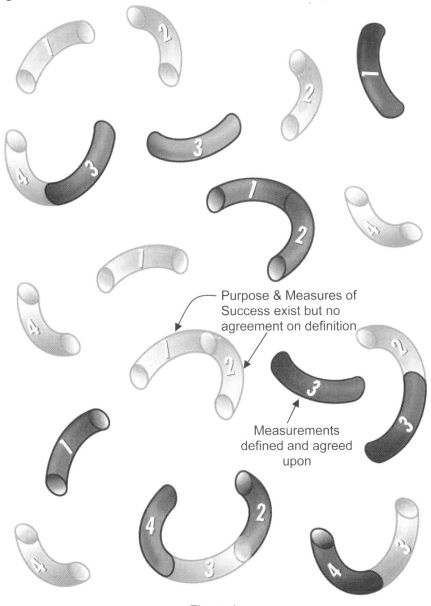

Purpose & Measures of Success exist but no agreement on definition

Measurements defined and agreed upon

Figure 1
Begin Pull Thinking
Establish present Pull link segments

Pull Thinking identifies missing, weak, and disconnected purposes and measures; measurements being taken that are not connected to a specific purpose or stated measure of success; ineffective frequency of measurement; and measurements in the wrong hands, where people are held accountable without direct authority to take action. Customers and suppliers often lack agreement; or where there is agreement; it is rare that all of the Pulls are complete and connected throughout the organization. This is misalignment, the source of chaos and added costs.

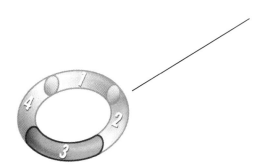

This Pull has only Question 3 answered. There is agreement on measurement. There is no connection to purpose, no Measures of Success, and no agreement on the frequency of measurements.

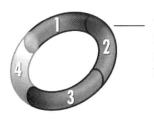

This Pull has Questions 1, 2, & 3 answered. Question 4 does not have agreement on the frequency of measurements.

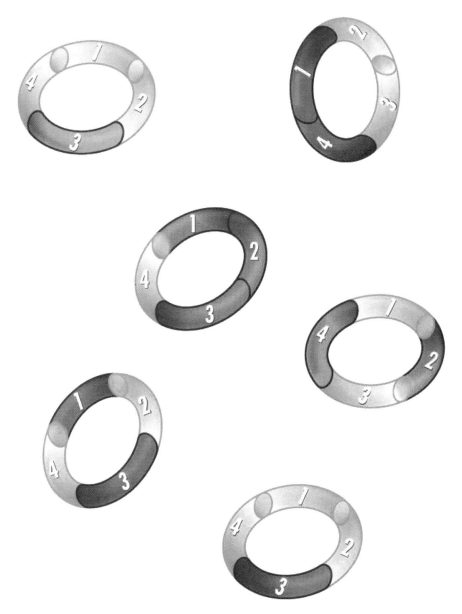

Figure 2
Identify all purposes—Pulls
create Pull links

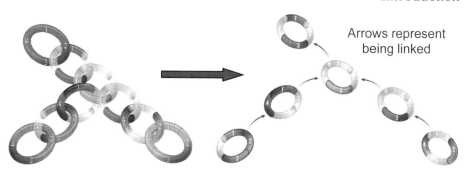

Arrows represent
being linked

Figure 3
Service Flow – Pull Structure
Customer – Supplier relationship & Service Flow Pull Structure established
Strategies being developed, unanswered Pull questions set priorities

3. The Pull Structure

We often do not follow through or go deep enough within an organization to utilize the effectiveness and power of purpose statements. The organization's missions and visions must be supported by and linked specifically to individuals, teams, departments and business units. Otherwise, missions and visions lose luster and passion over time.

When measurements and purposes are not well defined and not appropriately connected in a Pull Structure, many different strategies and seemingly unrelated problems and solutions float around. Our energies are not properly focused. As a result, problems or barriers seem hard to remove because the energy is weak. There are too many problems, too many fires to put out. It's hard to prioritize. The Four Pull Questions, together with a well-defined Pull Structure, enable Ultimate Service Flow bringing a laser focus on both priorities and solutions from the perspective of the whole process. Hence the <u>Pull Structure</u> will be referred to as the <u>Service Flow Pull Structure</u> throughout the the book.

This tool helps you build a solution that specifically identifies the steps that need to take place and the people to carry them out. No more ambiguity here. Instead, the Pull Structure delivers a disciplined strategy. One that creates a customer-focused culture, measurements of accountability and a clear-cut process that supports achievement and acknowledgement.

This is a visible, disciplined planning process. One that implements change and delivers a foundation for sustained success. In fact, it actually has more impact on the bottom line than any financial analysis or management system. With it, you can clearly see how every one is connected, the measurements that support achievement and the acknowledgement that reinforces performance.

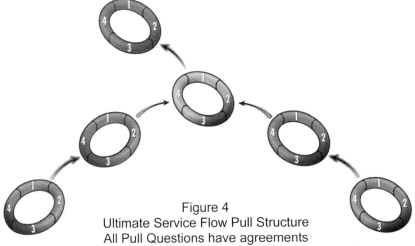

Figure 4
Ultimate Service Flow Pull Structure
All Pull Questions have agreements
The process of working toward Ultimate Service Flow has begun

The ultimate goal of Pull Thinking is to be in the process of achieving ultimate growth and learning to reach our full potential as an individual, team, and business by mastering the process of creating. A goal (the end state) needs to be chosen to serve as the vehicle for facilitating this process.

The goal of Pull Thinking in business is to <u>master the process of creating Ultimate Service.</u> In a Pull environment you will find people with purpose who have a passion for performance and provide service with integrity. Closing the gap between Figure 3 and Figure 4 results in reducing costs, improving quality, being on time, and high morale. All of which has a direct and positive affect on the bottom line. It is a laser focus on the leading measures of service processes that closes the gap…not the lagging financial measures on bottom line results.

The exciting aspect of Pull Thinking is that the process can start tomorrow (Condition 2. below); achieving the state of Ultimate Service Resonance (Condition 3. below) takes time. Achieving a goal like reaching the top of Mt. Everest requires a long disciplined process of training and skill development and yet we stand on the top for a brief moment in time. The process of getting stronger can start tomorrow and provides a learning that will last a lifetime.

The following three diagrams show the three conditions in the process of creating Ultimate Service Flow.

Condition 1. New problems are created and old problems are not addressed because there is little or no service flow—stagnation. In this condition problems fester until they become big enough to create emergencies or cause turbulence.

Condition 2. Problems are addressed and new problems are either prevented or quickly solved because there is service flow. The organization is in the process of creating Ultimate Service Flow. Sensitivity to problems increases as the flow of service increases.

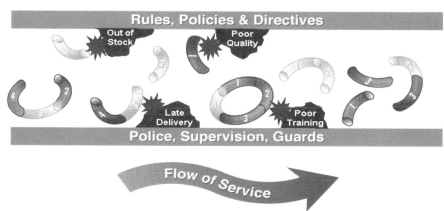

Condition 3. Problems do not exist and new problems are prevented because the organization has mastered the process of creating Ultimate Service Flow throughout the organization, there is Ultimate Service Resonance; the goal state of Pull Thinking.

Being in a Pull environment provides many opportunities:

- For customers, finding businesses with integrity of service.
- For employees, an energized, empowering work environment.
- For suppliers, attracting businesses to serve that resonate with their service.
- For company teams, learning to work together smoothly and efficiently.
- For investors, choosing the businesses with the highest probability of success.
- For mergers and acquisitions, increasing the probability of success and enabling the fastest integration with the least problems.
- For businesses, increased growth and profitability, as well as measures to clearly identify the high costs of service misalignments.
- For manufacturers, establishing the best context for implementing and sustaining a lean enterprise.
- For everyone, a compass that points to solutions and the best resources you need to create Ultimate Service.

What will you experience when you apply Pull Thinking?

- A natural approach to business that is clearly understood and supported by everyone, from the top floor where strategies are born to the "front lines"
- A universal language that links everyone and improves communication
- A clear vision supported by everyone throughout your organization
- An alignment between purpose and actions throughout your enterprise and supply chain creating Ultimate Service
- A clear understanding of responsibility
- The ability to understand the root cause of problems at lightning speed, accelerating improvement efforts
- Strategies and structures to create an energized learning environment and support new behaviors
- Required skills and tools are easily identified

Other technologies, improvement initiatives and tools that you may already know, such as Balanced Scorecard, Team Development, Six Sigma, Lean Enterprise, may come to mind as you read this. These are all excellent tools—there's no reason to forget what you know. Pull Thinking is compatible with all these other approaches; it simply provides a context upon which these tools become more powerful, a context that prevents failure.

Businesses today change the mindset of only a few people on a process improvement team. This may save money and time on training by not having to train everybody in an organization, but results in stressful implementations being <u>done to</u> those who have not changed how they think about their work. This is what happens in a level 2 change initiative as discussed in a recent McKinsey

Quarterly article regarding the psychology of change management and improving organizational performance.

"Over the past 15 or so years, programs to improve corporate organizational performance have become increasingly common. Yet they are notoriously difficult to carry out.

Success depends on persuading hundreds or thousands of groups and individuals to change the way they work, a transformation people will accept only if they can be persuaded to think differently about their jobs."

The Psychology of Change Management
Emily Lawson and Colin Price; *The McKinsey Quarterly, 2003 Number 2 Organization*

The article discusses three levels of change. Without level 3 being addressed, level 1 and 2 changes "are difficult to carry out." Summarized, the Pull Thinking context addresses level 3.

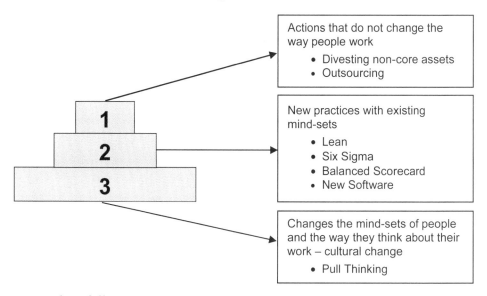

The following two diagrams depict the difference a Pull Thinking context can make. Level 1 and 2 changes are represented in the first diagram, and level 3 in the second diagram, with Pull Thinking as a foundation, support for improvement initiatives is enabled. By Harnessing the Power of Pull, you can dramatically improve and maximize the flow of communication, or of services, or of products.

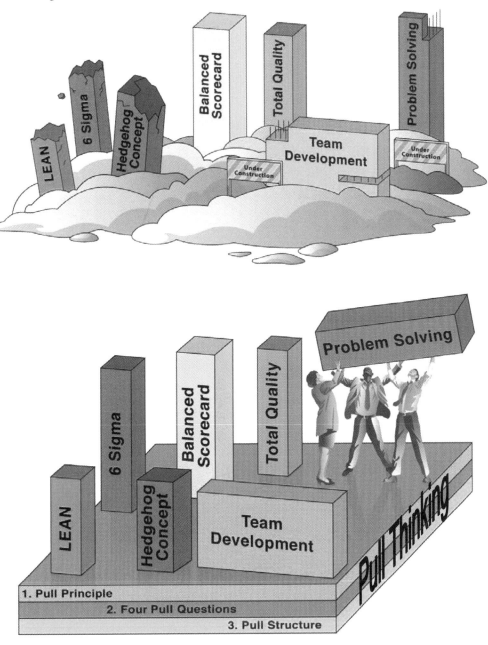

Here are some examples of Pull Thinking in action:

A consumer products manufacturer undertook a major initiative to train more than 300 associates in statistical process control (SPC). At the end of three years, no one is using SPC, and no one knows why. After applying Pull Thinking, the first SPC implementation takes place within eight weeks—with the full support of the union leaders and the hourly workers on the line.

A major aerospace subcontractor spent close to $500,000 and failed in their attempts to implement Total Quality Management, Just-in-Time, and demand flow manufacturing methods. Using Pull Thinking, a pilot team succeeded. Pull Thinking ensured union buy-in and within months, the team became the first certified "world-class" team within the $6 billion parent corporation.

A large cookware manufacturer in the Bronx was about to shutter a four-year-old consumer product line and lay-off employees because of ongoing and apparently insurmountable quality control problems. Using the tools in Pull Thinking, the company turned the situation around within a few weeks, and more than thirty jobs were saved.

A novice became the number one salesman at a men's clothing store, beating the pants off two 15-year veterans, by delivering Ultimate Service. He focused on the customers' needs, and developed an innovative way to hem pants to offer "quick alterations while you wait." Using Pull Thinking, the innovation came naturally. You'll read more about this and other examples in Step 7.

Is there a business case developing in your mind yet? Can you see a business case for implementing Pull Thinking taking shape for your organization?

About the organization of the book

This book is organized into Steps. Step One discusses the Pull Principle and explains the distinctions between Push and Pull. Step Two presents a simple mental model to show how Push and Pull impacts basic thought processes and the choices we make. Steps Three through Six provide details on each of the Four Pull Questions. Step Seven puts Pull Thinking into action.

Step Eight explores possibilities and opportunities after results begin to accumulate, provides practical application examples using Pull Thinking for continued improvement, and offers some "what's next" suggestions.

You'll find a simple flow chart at the beginning of each step. The information covered in each step is highlighted in the context of an integrated, one-page diagram showing all the basic aspects of the Pull Thinking process.

Keep in mind, though, that this isn't a cookbook. A cookbook provides you with recipes, with step-by-step instructions on how to, say, roast a chicken or whip up an eggplant soufflé. (There are, apparently, people who want to whip up eggplant soufflés.) But no matter how good the cookbook or its recipes are, it doesn't make you a chef. A chef knows how to combine ingredients and flavors to make traditional dishes or invent exciting new possibilities.

If you'll forgive the stretching of the metaphor just a bit, this book is designed to make you a master business chef. It doesn't teach you the step-by-step recipes to improve your office, your consultancy, your factory, your research lab, your department store, or your restaurant. But it will give you the tools and skills to create those recipes for yourself—and even to apply them elsewhere.

Step 1 —
The Pull Principle

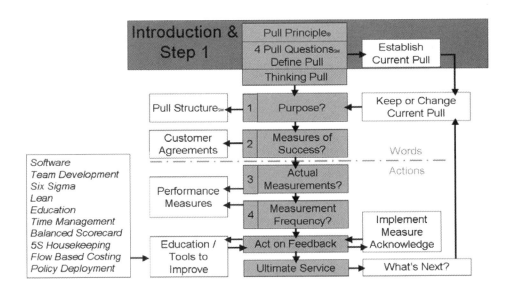

Pull Thinking Process

*"A prime mover that moves everything that is in motion
without moving and without itself being moved, must
cause motion by being attractive rather than propulsive."*
—Aristotle, 350 BC

It was true in 350 BC and it's still true today: the most effective way to cause any action is to work with its Pull. A prime mover without itself moving causes you to be motivated to move, to act, to create, or to grow.

> Pull Principle®
>
> Pull is the **Primary Force** that causes all movement.
> - Push is a response to Pull.
> - Pull is the most efficient way to create, grow, and improve – anything. Everything.
> - Pull is Nature's creative force. No one can avoid or alter it.

Tenet 1. Pull is the primary force that causes all movement. Push is a response to Pull.

If this is true, it means that Pull is the fundamental creative force in nature that causes all movement, actions and other forces. It would mean that only a Pull force can create a Push force. Why would that be important to know? How would we benefit?

If I wanted to know how or why something is moving or being created, I would first look to find what is Pulling; what Pull force is at work. Scientists study the how and why in nature everyday in order to learn how to improve our lives.

It didn't surprise me when I read about words like "strange attractor," "magnet," and Pull used to describe some of the latest discoveries by scientists trying to understand the process that produces complexities and chaos in nature. Scientists gave the name "Strange Attractor" to the source of chaos in the universe. The "order in chaos" was uncovered.

The attractor—the simplest kind possible—is like a pinpoint magnet embedded in a rubber sheet.[7]" What does a magnet do? *It Pulls*! This fact led scientists to another question about this pinpoint: "how can all the information about a complicated system be stored in a point?" There's a complicated mathematical answer, but the scientists explain it to the rest of us this way:

> "We do not need the equations of motion to know the destiny of a pendulum subject to friction. Every orbit must eventually end up at the same place, the center: position 0, velocity 0. This central fixed point "attracts" the orbits. Instead of looping around forever, they spiral inward. The friction dissipates the system's energy, and in phase space the dissipation shows itself as a pull toward the center, from the outer regions of high energy to the inner regions of low energy. The attractor—the simplest kind possible—is like a pinpoint magnet embedded in a rubber sheet.
>
> One advantage of thinking of states as points in space is that it makes change easier to watch."

Their words "…pull toward the center," "The attractor…is like a pinpoint magnet," "…thinking of states as points…makes change easier to watch" support the Pull Principle. They're saying that states or conditions are being "Pulled" into creation by strange attractors.

This discovery was a result of a change in how scientists measured complexity and chaos. They were looking too closely at

---

[7] James Gleick, *Chaos: Making a New Science*, Penguin Books, 1987, page 134

the problem. Only when they learned how to "step back" did they begin to see that chaos is a simple point in time, a state in a process. By stepping back, they began to see order as the source of chaos.

Chaos was either decreasing as an end state (order) approached or increasing as a destruction process (disorder) progressed. To put it in a simple example, instead of measuring once every second and seeing the same state of chaos, they changed the measurement frequency to once every week and still saw chaos, but a different chaos. Using these differences, the changes in state, scientists were able to project the end state. This revealed the order within the process.

With Pull Thinking, we can "step back" and make the "strange attractor" less strange, because the pinpoint Pull of the magnet in the center of the rubber sheet can be identified. How? Simple. By establishing the answer to all Four Pull Questions: a purpose, measures of success, measurements, and frequency of measurements.

The primary Pull force is responsible for the structure of Pulls needed to create the end state (as you progress through this book you'll see that in business, end state refers to the ultimate order—the flow of Ultimate Service). One can understand how all the information about a business can be stored in a single point when that point is the primary Pull, the Pull of the customer.

The complex structure of an organization, the DNA, can be determined by one pinpoint, by a few simple rules. We have only to understand Pull in order to begin the process of seeing what to change and how to change it. For any type of service your organization chooses to provide, there is a structure, an Ultimate Service Flow Pull Structure, waiting to be Pulled into existence.

The difference between a Pull environment and a Push environment is obvious. In a Pull environment, people know what is Pulling and understand the reason for any Push. There are only appropriate Push forces, those that improve the flow and support the primary Pull. In a Push environment, people do not clearly know what is Pulling. The process and end state is not clear and Push forces are often inappropriate. It is chaotic and disorganized in comparison to a Pull environment. To those not having experienced a Pull environment it seems normal, as if there is nothing wrong.

So, why would it be important to know Pull? How would we benefit? The obvious answer is: the more we know about the process of how things work, how things get created, the more we can improve upon what we do, what we create.

If what we do is provide service, then the best service, Ultimate Service, would be the goal for any business. Therefore, WHAT we need to do is PULL. HOW this is done is a process of using the Four Pull Questions, together with Pull Structures, to create an Ultimate Service Flow process.

If the desire to improve is part of our human DNA and people are what businesses are made of, it's in the DNA of business. The first place to begin, the most efficient place, the place where one has the highest leverage, and the most economical place, is in our thinking.

The next step, Step 2, uses a mental model approach to show how Push and Pull forces work in our thought processes. But first, more about the Pull Principle and the distinctions between Push and Pull.

So what is a Pull force?

From Webster's dictionary[8] we see the positive nature of Pull:

Pull/verb/
> 1: to draw the support or attention of
> 2: to exert force upon so as to cause or tend to cause motion toward the force
> 3: Pull one's weight: to do one's full share of the work — pull together — to work in harmony.

Pull/noun/
> 1: a force that attracts, compels, or influences: Attraction

[8] Simon & Schuster, Inc., © 1994, *Webster's New World Dictionary®, Third College Edition*

What does Pull sound like?

Listen carefully to people's words, and when you hear phrases like these, they're describing a Pull force in their life:

- A passion for…
- Inspired by…
- Feel compelled to…
- Attracted to…
- Focused on…
- In the zone…

- Consumed by…
- Caught up in…
- High need to…
- Want to…
- Interested in…
- Can't wait to…

These are the words you'll hear from people working in the top 100 places to be employed. That's not a coincidence.

A Pull force is the attraction you feel, for example, for that new Lexus in the showroom. Think about how it draws you inside and compels you to want to buy. The Pull of the Lexus resonates with something inside you and causes you to move toward it (literally and figuratively). Notice, however, that the Lexus itself is not in motion. It's not doing anything.

The pirate gold in *Treasure Island* is the Pull—it *Pulls* the characters into the action of the story. It's the primary motivator. But it doesn't do anything in the story. It doesn't push anyone out of the door of the inn and onto the ship. It simply waits.

There is always a Pull.

In short, Pull attracts or causes you to be motivated to take action. Common sense tells us that the most powerful way to effect the motivation in others is to understand what attracts, motivates, or delights them. When everyone responds with complete and total integrity (you can't <u>not</u> act with integrity in a Pull environment) the result is Ultimate Service Resonance.

Think of what it means when someone says:
"I don't want to *push* that."
"Stop *pushing* me; I'll do it when I'm ready."
"We're really *pushed* to get though this project."
"Stop *pushing* my buttons."

Now think what it means to say:
>"Let's *pull* together and get this done."
>"We *pulled* it out in the end!"
>"I'm *pulling* for you all the way."
>"I was *pulled* in!"

It turns out that we instinctively know when we are experiencing a Pull and when we are experiencing a Push. "He's pushy." "She helped me pull it all together." A Pull is an attraction like gravity. Pull facilitates natural flow.

What about Push?

The Dictionary definition of Push: [9]

Push/verb/
1: to press against with force in order to drive or impel
2: to bear hard upon so as to involve in difficulty
3: to exert oneself continuously, vigorously, or obtrusively to gain an end

Push/*noun*
1: a vigorous effort, campaign, etc.
2: an advance against opposition
3: pressure of affairs or of circumstances
4: an emergency
5: [Colloq.] aggressiveness; enterprise; drive

Perhaps in the future another definition will be added:
>"6: the result of a Pull."

---

[9] Simon & Schuster, Inc., © 1994, *Webster's New World Dictionary®, Third College Edition*

If Push is a force exerted in opposition to and is a result of a Pull force, it follows that if there is no Pulling, there can be no Pushing.

Remember, you're not going to row upstream (push) unless you have a good reason—a Pull. We may appropriately push to overcome someone's resistance (push back) to our request; or we may appropriately push to make something happen. We have to push to get our canoe upstream. Is push bad? It depends on the purpose or Pull creating the Push. Push that improves the flow, resolves problems or prevents problems is appropriate.

In a Push environment, there is inappropriate Push—it impedes the flow. People work at causing problems whether knowingly or not. As a manager in a Push environment, you control, administer, direct, and, well, push. At the end of the day, you're stressed out and hassled from trying to get everyone to do what you want.

Think of a project manager dealing with an employee who never gets his work done on time. He is an obstacle in the service flow, rather than a facilitator. While the rest of the team is working to clear the path of the stream (so that service flows optimally) he is like a rock that causes turbulence.

Today, the tardy employee wants to go home early—it's such nice golfing weather outside.

The project manager frowns. "You *must* get this work done before you go home tonight."

The employee argues, insisting that the project manager is being unreasonable, since the work is not due until 10 am the next day.

Who's going to win this argument? Probably the manager—the work will get done before the employee laces up his golf shoes. However, the interaction is not very pleasant and takes a lot of effort on the manager's part. The project manager pushed the employee and "won," but she had a very unpleasant experience. She's not happy; even though she now knows the work will be done on time; and the employee is certainly not happy.

A better way is to find a way to Pull the employee into line with the rest of the team—to make him understand his role in the accomplishment of the goals (the Pull) of the team, and how his actions impact the others. If he wants to be rewarded (by, say, being able to leave early now and again) he needs to contribute to the team's Pull of Ultimate Service. Performance, in other words, needs to become the Pull.

Let's think of the employee as a sailor. If he doesn't pull his line to set his sail when the others do, the boat doesn't move as it should. It's off course. It looses speed. It could even sail into disaster. His individual Pull may not seem important to him, but to the captain (or project manager) who sees the course, the action is critical.

Unless we change our thinking and our approach, we're likely to repeat these types of unpleasant, "just get things done or else" warnings. The question is: what might the project manager have done differently?

She might have stopped to wonder why there is a Push here. If she had, she might have realized that the Push really stems from her desire to make sure the employee gets the work done ahead of time, which is crucial to his learning a lesson and her peace of mind. Notice however, that in her push to get the work done before the employee goes home, the underlying motivation for our actions is not communicated to the employee.

If there is action, there must be Pull—but there may or may not be any Pushing. For action to occur, the Pull force must be greater than the Push force. The effort to make the employee finish must be greater than his inertia—his desire not to work.

In this example, if the employee wants to leave early to play golf more than he wants to keep the manager happy, he may soon not have a job at all. Sure, he'll have time to play golf, but he won't have the green to pay the green fee. More, the project manager will have to find and train a replacement without sacrificing productivity. Who's winning here?

In a Pull environment, the employee would learn to share the team's Pull—like in the cover illustration, he would want to sail into calmer waters. He would understand that when the entire team functions together, the boat moves as it should. When he consistently accomplishes his tasks properly and on time, he is in the Pull of the team. The boat sails into calmer, sunlit seas. And the manager can stop pushing him. He may even get to play a few more rounds of golf. In short, everyone wins.

Do you ever wonder why supervisors push employees to do something? It is *always* because there is something that is *Pulling* them. In our example, the project manager is trying to push the employee to complete a project task. The Pull for the project manager is the desire to get projects done on time, one of the measures of her success. Since her success depends on the work her employees do, she's under a great deal of stress when her employees wait until the last minute.

Now, the employee *wants* to contribute, but contributing is the best way to obtain his own goals. When the team wins, he wins. Now, the manager is Pulling, not Pushing. The resistance is gone.

What does Push sound like?

- Pushed by…
- Have to…
- Forced to…
- Pressured by…
- Hassled by…
- Reluctantly…
- Told to…
- No choice but to…
- Arm-twisted to…
- Required by…
- Stressed out about…
- Against my better judgment…

These are the words you'll more commonly hear from people in business today. Knowing when Push is appropriate is key.

Example: The chronically late employee

Let's examine this a little further.

An employee routinely arrives late to work, causing disruption for your business. You can get angry and insist that the person show up on time. You can fire the employee if there is no improvement. However, firing him will result in going through the process, expense, and hassle of hiring and training someone new. Nobody wins in that situation.

As an alternative, you can discuss the problem and find out why the tardy behavior is occurring. In Pull Thinking terms, you would try to identify what is causing this person to be late. Perhaps the cause is a transportation problem. If you suggest a solution, you would have improved the situation from a customer service point of view.

What you really need is for the employee to be proactive and take responsibility for being on time. Only then could you say that the employee is in the Pull of the customer. The manager, then, wouldn't have to keep pushing (or threatening); the employee would be pulled, just like you are pulled into that Lexus dealership.

So what are the alternatives? Threatening (pushing) doesn't eliminate any problems. In fact, by increasing stress, it may even cause *new* problems. The trick is to ensure that the employee understands his role, and why it is critical to the success of the team as a whole. When the team wins, he wins. Now, he has a Pull (rather than the push of a threat) to perform.

The manager, likewise, knows that the team's success depends upon everyone's contributions. She knows that for everyone to succeed, she must enable his success. If she can remove the barriers that prevent him from contributing, (by arriving on time) everyone wins. She accomplishes more by Pulling than Pushing.

Note that in this example, she's coaching, not micromanaging. Using our sailing metaphor again, she doesn't tell the team which lines to Pull to move the sails; she simply communicates the purpose—sets the course, knowing that the team will do what is required to turn the boat.

With Pull Thinking, the project manager has a choice. She can exert a lot of energy dealing with this issue, or she can have the employee take responsibility himself. Obviously, it's much easier if the employee can handle getting to work on time without the manager's intervention. So how could she know ahead of time if the employee is in the Pull of the customer?

Pull Thinking answers that question, because it uncovers the Pull forces present. As a result, it enables appropriate action to change or realign the Pull forces to bring about better results by preventing problems.

Continuing our example, the employee is still late and the manager has asked to see him to discuss the situation and applies Pull Thinking:

> **Manager**: "The purpose of this business is to serve our customers. One of the Measures of Success in support of this purpose is that each member of the team, including you, be at work on time every day." (This is the purpose and one of the Measures of Success.)

Note that the manager clearly states the Measure of Success in her (vision/mission) purpose statement.

> **Manager**: "The time you arrive is recorded everyday. If you are unable to be on time, you need to let us know in advance so that we can arrange for someone else to take your place until you can be here." This is the measurement and frequency: on time (yes or no) and everyday.

Note that the manager clearly states the actual measurement and frequency of measurement.

One way to access the Pull of the employee would be to ask these questions to define and understand his Measures of Success for being on time.

> 1. When is being late okay?
>   - every day
>   - occasionally
>   - only if it is unavoidable — in an emergency
>   - other
> 2. If I (the manager) have a problem with your being late, what are you most likely to do?
>   - show up when you can and apologize for being late
>   - call as soon as you realize that you will be late

- ask for help to solve your problems
- solve the problem and show up on time
- other

3. If you know that you (the employee) have a problem with being on time, are you most likely to?
   - continue being late until you're fired
   - accept the fact that you are unable to be on time and quit the job
   - look for a job where being late is okay
   - do what it takes to be on time
   - other

These questions access the employee's Measures of Success—provided the employee has integrity and tells the truth. His answers will show the alignment of his Pull force regarding being on time in relation to the customer's (or manager's) Pull force. The final step is to write the four parts of the Pull force down (the Four Pull Questions), which allows everyone involved to clearly see the Pull force in black and white.

Once that happens, the next steps become obvious.

Integrity matters—actions speak louder than words

The Four Pull Questions work together to ensure system integrity.

To succeed in a Pull environment, you need to have two things: 1) all the information, and 2) integrity. If a customer does not tell you their Measures of Success, then a clear Pull may not be known until after a misstep during a trial and error process. If a customer says one thing but means another, then *integrity of purpose* is not established and a breakdown of service may be eminent.

The same goes for the employee. Communication is the thread that connects the supplier and customer. Asking the right questions ensures alignment between their Measures of Success. It is this alignment that ensures that the supplier is in the Pull of the customer. There is service with integrity.

However, if the manager fails to actually measure being on time every day as he said he would, his integrity of action is not in alignment with the purpose.

The moral of the chronically late employee example:

What the manager said:	What the manager did:	What it means to the employee:
Being on time every day is really important	Measures being on time only when a problem occurs.	Not causing a problem is really important

Integrity problem here	Creates integrity problem here

What works better?

Manager says:	Manager does:	What it means to the employee:
Being on time every day is really important	Measures being on time _every_ day	Being on time every day is really important

Integrity here	Creates integrity here

Understanding the distinction and the relationship, between Push and Pull can add meaning for everyone in your organization. The second tenet of the Pull Principle adds to this importance.

Tenet 2. Pull is the most efficient way to create, grow, and improve – anything. Everything.

If Pull causes all movement, why wouldn't it be the most efficient way to create something? When you consider this to be true and look around for evidence, you'll find plenty. The water flowing downstream in the pull of gravity can generate power. It requires a great deal of energy to push water up a pipe. A boat sailing downstream requires less power than a boat sailing against the current. These are perhaps oversimplified examples, but the idea here is important: It's easier to go with flow, to be in the Pull, than to push against the flow.

There is evidence of the efficiency of Pull all around us:

- Gravity is a Pull force.
- Magnetism and electricity are Pull forces.
- Front-wheel-drive cars and trains are Pulled.
- Magnet schools Pull students to learn.
- Powerful, shared visions Pull organizations together.
- The human biological system is a Pull system.

Here are characteristics of Push and Pull environments from different perspectives. See if you can recognize these characteristics from your own experiences:

In a <u>Push environment</u>, people do not clearly know what is Pulling. The end state is not clear and Push forces are inappropriate.

In a <u>Pull environment</u> people know what is Pulling and understand the reason for any Push. There are only appropriate Push forces.

Push <u>Business Perspective</u> **Pull**

- Maximizing utilization of resources
- Many measures in the hands of a few
- Lack of context for measurements
- Difficult for the greatness in people to come out

- Maximizing the flow of service & resources to customers
- Few measures in the hands of many
- A clear context for measurements
- Natural for the greatness in people to come out

Primary focus = Profit
Results:

- Dissatisfied customers
- Unhappy employees
- High employee turnover
- Non-value added work
- Dwindling profits long term
- Make & Sell

Primary focus = Customer
Results:

- Satisfied customers
- Passionate employees
- Greater employee loyalty
- Lean enterprise
- Long term growth of profits
- Sense & Respond

Push <u>Communication Perspective</u> **Pull**

- Measures of Success known after the fact
- I know only what is in my black box
- Top down
- Secrets

- Measures of Success known before the fact
- Everyone is on the same page & sees the big picture
- Bottom up
- Transparent

In a Push environment, empty time gets filled, because the focus is on maximizing the utilization of the resources. Many people unknowingly work at less than 100 percent efficiency, resulting in time and space that is filled with inefficient or non-value added actions. Busy work. The goal is to find the empty space that has been filled with non-purposeful activity.

Some additional questions may come to mind at this point. Ask them, and be prepared to listen carefully for the answers as you progress through the book, even if (or especially if) the answers aren't what you expect.

- How do you find the inefficient and wasteful actions?
- What Pulls the space to be filled with non-purposeful activity? (Why do people feel they have to look busy? How is their activity impacting others?)
- Why isn't there a Pull to eliminate non-purposeful activity?
- If there is a Pull to eliminate the non-purposeful activity, why isn't it being done?
- If the non-purposeful activity is hidden, why is it hidden?
- What are the causes and effects?

The answers to these questions will become apparent as we progress through the steps in this book.

People with a manufacturing background are familiar with the difference between a Push System and a Pull System: in a Push System, material is released (pushed) into the manufacturing process, regardless of whether or not there is current demand (or machine capacity) for the product. In contrast, in a Pull System, the strong Pull of the customer is used to initiate all actions in the plant, and the work flows through the process "just in time." The customer's needs are met, but nothing is warehoused, or must wait for the next point in the "production area" to be ready. Costs are reduced, the distribution chain is streamlined, and everything works more efficiently. A few typical results often realized from implementing Pull Systems and Flow in manufacturing are:

- Quality levels go from a high level of rejects to a very low level of rejects
- Inventory costs are reduced by 90% or more
- Space needed to produce products is reduced by 50% to 80%
- Employee morale greatly improves, turnover decreases

When working with Pull, there are fewer problems, less stress, more integrity, more passion, more efficiency, more growth, more connectedness, more improvement...it's just better.

Tenet 3. Pull is nature's creative force. No one can avoid or alter it.

Gravity is the attractive force in the physical world. It Pulls you down to earth and provides a nice, breathable atmosphere. You can't avoid it, any more than you can avoid the attraction of Pull.

If a physical object hits or pushes another physical object, is the source a Pull force or a Push force? The obvious answer seems to be a Push, but that's because we're looking too closely. From a higher perspective, we can see what happened first. Something first *pulled* them to want to *push*. In a baseball game, the bat pushed the ball, but the batter swung the bat in response to his own Pulls—his desire to win the game, for cheers from the fans, for a new contract, or just to impress his wife. Ultimately, there is a Pull involved, whether we feel it, talk about it, or choose to work with it. Again, if Push is a force exerted in opposition to or in response to a Pull force, it follows that without Pull, there is no Push. There is always a Pull. You cannot avoid it. Since we cannot avoid it, why not work with it?

Pull creates flow, not Push, where there is flow, there is Pull

To continue with the stream example, think of the flow of service as a stream, as in the following diagram. Water flowing in a stream is Pulled by the force of gravity (which can be equated to customer Pull in a service flow). The rocks in the stream (problems) cause resistance to the flow (of service), which means they're pushing against the flow. The result is turbulence (issues and problems) and chaos in the water.

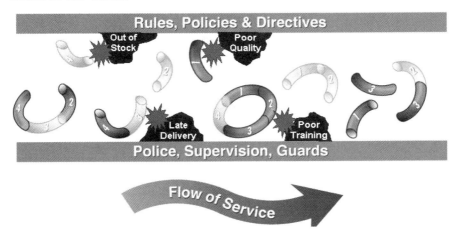

With this thought in mind, Push has a purpose—to be a signal, to create turbulence—to respond to the Pull. Seeing the turbulence we can find the problem—the rock in the stream—push it away to improve the flow. Without flow, there is no reason to respond.

If a dam was built, the flow would stop, the water would be still, the push from the rocks would stop, and the turbulence and chaos would disappear. No flow, no push, no chaos. The problems are hidden, waiting to be discovered.

In this metaphor, good service "stops." But poor service trickles over the spillway and into the tributaries, which fill up from the push back of the dam. This causes customers to go out of their way to get water, or service, instead of the water or service coming to them downstream. The customer must now go upstream to the tributaries to get the water that should flow to them.

To see another example of flow, imagine a string of beads on a table. If we push on the beads, all the beads will pile up in a chaotic way. To eliminate the chaotic pile, we would need to use all of our fingers to push and sort, and sustain order as we push the beads forward, each finger representing management Push. Or, we can simply let the customer pull on the first bead until all the beads are lined up and flowing in orderly response to the customers Pull.

In both cases we can move the beads, but only by pulling do we create an orderly flow from chaos with the least effort. Notice also that pulling on the first bead with a quick stop and start motion will result in an immediate identical stop and start motion with the rest of the beads. It's faster and there are lower costs. This is an example of excellent communication between the beads with each bead transferring the Pull force through to the following bead. They are all linked! It is an Ultimate Service Flow environment, a Pull environment.

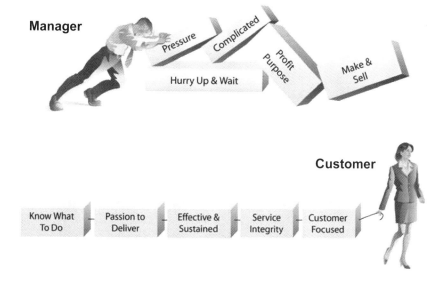

In an Ultimate Service Flow environment, the most perfect sustained orderly flow with the least effort is the result of the "primary mover"—the primary Pull of the customer.

From her award-winning best-selling book *Leadership and the New Science*, listen to what Margaret J. Wheatley has to say regarding the new science of chaos:

> "In chaos theory it is true that you can never tell where the system is headed until you've observed it over time. Order emerges, but it doesn't materialize instantly. This is also true for organizations, and this is a great challenge in our speed-crazed world. It takes time to see that a well-centered organization really has enough invisible structure to work well. Many of these organizations are already out there, beckoning to us from the future. But if they have not been part of our own experience, we are back to acts of faith. As the universe keeps revealing more of its ordering processes, hopefully we will understand that systems achieve order from clear centers rather than imposed restraints."
>
> Margaret J. Wheatley[10]

---

[10] Wheatley, Margaret J., *Leadership and the New Science*, 1999, page 132

Step 2
Thinking Pull

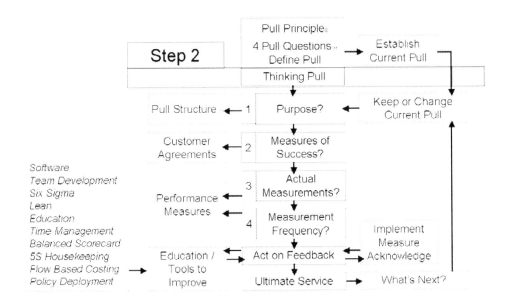

Pull Thinking Process

"Man's mind, once stretched by a new idea,
never regains its original dimensions."
— Oliver Wendell Holmes

"...by far the most powerful force of attraction in organizations and in our
lives is meaning."
— Margaret J. Wheatley

So how do we Harness the Power of Pull?

We do it by the use of the tools of Pull Thinking: the Pull
Principle, the Four Pull Questions, and the Pull Structure. But
before we discuss these tools in detail, we need to understand how
Push and Pull work in our thought process, our thinking, and our
minds. With the simple language of Pull Thinking it is easy to form a
new context and change culture, motivation and behavior. Knowing
why we need to change eases the fear of change. This step is
important because it addresses why Pull Thinking works. It also
addresses that strongest attractor in each of us: our ego—our
identity.

We all work in many different types of organizations, large and
small, serving customers in many different ways. Whether you wear
a blue collar, white collar, or are a doctor, an athlete, a politician, an
educator, an artist, a scientist, or an executive, there is one thing we
all have in common besides serving customers, communicating,
wanting to find meaning, and wanting to grow, it is—thinking.

Weeks following one of the first seminars that I gave in 1989,
one of the participants called me over when I was shopping at the
store where she worked and proceeded to tell me about her
experience when she discussed Pull Thinking with her fiancé. He
was a very successful real-estate developer. As she explained Pull

Thinking to him, his eyes began to light up as he listened. He said, "you know, what you are saying is exactly how I think. I have never heard anyone describe that to me."

This is exactly why Step 2 exists. We all Pull but do not know how to Harness the Power of Pull. The language of Pull Thinking allows us to step back and see our thought processes at work. It cuts through the normal "fix it" mentality. It is the soft part, and often avoided part of managing an organization; because thinking is not in the objective realm where bottom line, fact-based decisions are made.

Pull Thinking starts with knowing how our minds operate

Years ago, you could buy a clock mounted on a comical picture of two farm children playing with a red wagon. Maybe you remember it. The child pulling the wagon is looking back at his brother asking: "Are you pushin' or pullin' back there?" Even at that age, it's important to know what's going on.

It's important to recognize how our minds are Pulled—what attracts, motivates, excites, and delights us. We are built to need to know "Why?" We want to find meaning.

Everyone has different experiences and backgrounds, as well as different learning styles and rates—we are all unique. Our individual needs Pull us in different directions at different times. Sometimes, we are pulled by physical needs—food, shelter, and clothing. Other times, it is by social needs—to be recognized and appreciated. But sometimes we are pulled by something higher—the need to grow and create. This need is present in all of us, all the time. It's hardwired into our very DNA; it's at the very core of our human design.

As individuals, we grow by mastering new skills through experience. That's a Pull. As part of this experience, we must give of ourselves, do the work, and expend energy to become more than we already are. Just like a business, we constantly have many opportunities to put forth effort. It is in pursuit of these experiences that individuals grow. In these experiences, we add new knowledge, skills, and beliefs.

Let's take that idea one step further. The foundation of any business is its people. Consequently, the model for business growth begins with the model for individual growth. How does that work? Let's take a look, beginning with the diagram below.

A model for growth

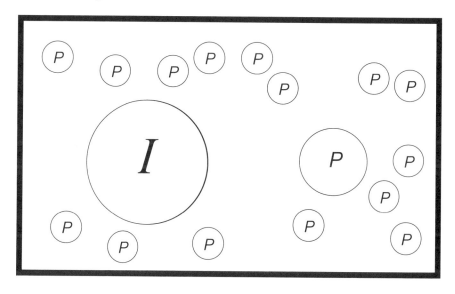

In the diagram, The "IDENTITY" circle (*I*), represents part of our mind. It encompasses *what we know we know*. It includes the background of knowledge from our history and experiences, including what we remember and have forgotten. It is all that we are at any given point in time. It's a pretty big circle.

The "POSSIBILITY" circles (*P*), represent another part of our mind: *what we know we don't know*. Possibilities are visions of the future, opportunities for learning, creating new memories, and forging new connections. If you don't speak French, the French language might be a possibility circle. You know you don't know it now, but you have the possibility of learning it if you have the desire (Pull) and you put forth the appropriate effort.

Take Fred for example, a hypothetical project manager for a residential construction company. Fred does a great job managing the construction of homes—one home at a time. His company recognizes his potential, and offers him the chance to manage their newest project, the concurrent construction of five homes.

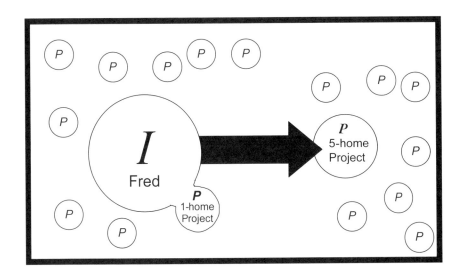

In the diagram above, the largest circle, I, represents Fred's identity. The remaining circles represent Fred's possibilities. He already has the skill to complete a one-home project, so that's already a part of his identity.

When Fred is interested in a specific possibility, there will be a Pull force that attracts him. This Pull force is a function of his individual needs, interests and experiences. Fred is excited about this project, because of the opportunity it represents for his professional growth.

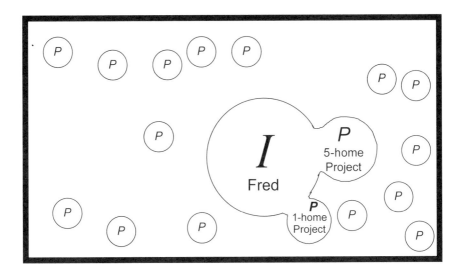

The Pull force on Fred will ensure that he puts his energy into successfully delivering those five homes in a way that will please his customers.

His actions will show that he is clearly in the Pull of fulfilling this newly chosen possibility.

Fred knows his purpose for the project and has the means to gain the experience…all that's left is for him to actually do the work.

As a result of giving of himself to provide service, Fred's identity grows. This larger area represents his new identity, expanded by his growth. He has now incorporated the new experience and skills he gained from the project into his identity.

Notice that he actually *had to build the five homes* (only *action* counts) to have the *P* become part of his identity.

It's just like exercising. If Fred started lifting weights, his muscles would become stronger and larger. They would have more capability.

The same is true of Fred's identity when he learns the new skill. Now his identity circle is larger—he has greater capacity for achievement—because he was Pulled to put forth effort to grow.

> *"...the task was no longer separate from the self... but rather he identified with this task so strongly that you couldn't define his real self without including that task."*
> — Dr. Abraham Maslow,
> Expert on human behavior and motivation

Think of how many people introduce them selves by stating what they do—"I'm a sales manager."

"I'm a baseball player."

"I'm a parent."

"I'm a scientist."

"I'm an author."

"I'm a CEO."

Our abilities shape our function, and our function helps shape our identity.

What else is contained within the box?

Everything else in the box besides Fred's identity (*I*) and all of the possibilities (*P*) represents all that Fred can create and become: his potential. It is what *he doesn't know he doesn't know*—the source of the continuous new possibilities life has in store for him.

As Fred's *I* grows, it fills in more and more of his potential. As human beings, we are programmed to grow and reach our full potential. In that sense, we're like the Blob in that old movie.

We consume more, and we grow larger and more capable, in a positive and non-destructive sort of way. It's our Pull.

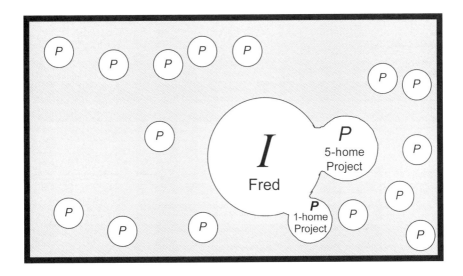

Growing is also risky

The risk inherent in growth is always present in our minds. Each of us, however, has different tolerances for risk that affect our willingness to go outside of ourselves in pursuit of various possibilities. That's why some of us are satisfied with a new Lexus, while others are compelled to climb Mount Everest. We have different Pulls.

For Fred to grow, he will have to have new experiences. His *I* circle needs to encompass more *P* circles.

If he does not go outside of his *I*, he will not have new challenges. He will not grow. It is a risk for Fred to take on the project to build the five homes, because he hasn't had that experience before. He might fail.

Although he is excited about the possibility for growth, he is comfortable doing what he knows he does well. He is very unlikely to fail if he stays in his comfort zone—if he keeps on building one house at a time. He doesn't know that he will be successful managing the 5-home project. He fears the consequences of failure.

It's natural to fear the unknown. That fear, too, is hardwired into our DNA. This fear is what could keep him from expanding his horizons, because it is safer to simply stay as he is. His *I* is pulling him back into himself. The *I* always wants to protect itself.

"*With meaning as our attractor, we can recreate ourselves to carry forward what we value most.*"[1] Margaret J. Wheatley

---

[1] Margaret J. Wheatley, *Leadership and the New Science*, Berrett-Koehler Publishers, 1999, pg 134

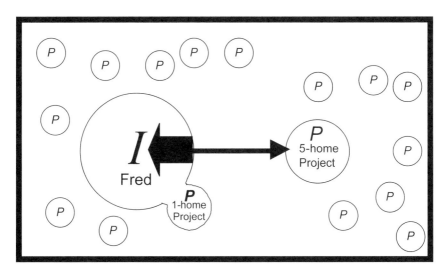

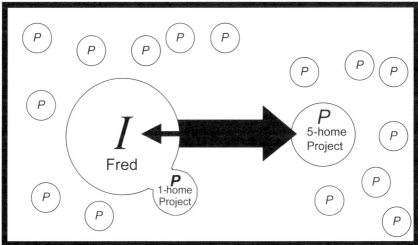

The bigger the apparent risk, the greater the fear, the greater the Pull of the *I* to protect itself. However, the urge to grow is also a powerful Pull. How does Fred decide? He has to determine which is the greater Pull—safety or the opportunity to grow. If the benefit of the *P* outweighs the risk to the *I*, then Fred will have an easier time choosing to pursue it. The "growth Pull overpowers the "protect Pull."

Asking "Why" reduces the fear of growth

By asking the question "Why?" our pal Fred can gain more knowledge and reduce the fear that his actions may result in negative consequences. This makes it easier to be pulled outside of his *I* and have the opportunity to grow.

What holds us back from growing?

As human beings, we have a finite amount of energy—mental and physical. At any one time, we may be pulled in different, sometimes opposite directions. It is the strength of the pull that determines which one absorbs the most energy. Not all pulls offer the possibility of growth.

Besides fear of the unknown, there are many other pulls that get in the way of growth. Some of the major ones are:

- Personal problems
- Personality issues
- Fear of failure
- Unhappiness
- Money and financial needs

These and other pulls will cause team members and co-workers to divert some of their energy in directions that diminish their ability to grow and to serve others.

In a Pull context, growth happens in three ways:

1) *The Pull of a new possibility* is the force that Pulls us to stretch beyond our current identity, and take the risks required to learn something new—to fulfill more of our potential. This is the most comfortable way to grow. It's natural.

2) *The Push from someone else* (our boss, team members, customers, etc.) can force or motivate us toward the possibility. For a Push force to exist there must first be an underlying Pull force. Once you identify the Pull force on the person who is pushing you, you can

choose to be in their Pull force or not, and accept the consequences. Your life may be easier if you choose to be in their Pull instead of resisting.

3) *The Push from ourselves* is the force we exert to remove the Pull of other needs so that we can be in the Pull we choose. For example, we push ourselves to work through lunch to prepare for an important business meeting instead of going out with friends. Or, we request a push from someone else, like a personal fitness trainer, to support our Pull to be fit.

Since Pull is more efficient and comfortable than Push, growth thrives in a Pull environment.

Push Environment	**Pull Environment**
Complaints	Requests
I have little choice	I do have a choice
Stressful & complicated	Fulfilling & uncomplicated
No clear purpose	My purpose is clear

There is a big difference between Pushing ourselves and being Pushed. Pushing ourselves comes from a strong and desirable Pull on us—something out there is very attractive to us, Pulling us to behave, make choices, and take actions that support growth.

When Pushed by others, we spend energy resisting, resulting in complication and stress. We have problems with being responsible or accountable. We often justify being in a Push environment by simply claiming we have nowhere else to go. If it gets really bad, we quit. The cause of high employee turnover in business has deep roots in Push. When purposes are not clear, we either find ourselves being pulled in different directions with little possibility for growth or we create our own Pulls causing the need for being managed.

We are more familiar with Push than Pull

Let's face it—most people have a lifetime history of Pushing and being Pushed.

We are accustomed to Push, because so much of our learning came from trial and error processes where measures of success are known only after the fact. Think of a child who learns not to touch a hot pot on the stove by being burned. Afterwards, the measure of success is: *not* being burned when touching something hot. Before, he had no knowledge or experience to know of that measure. That's a little over-simplified, but you get the idea.

Learning the measures of success by trial and error often results in corrections by others if we misbehaved, whether we intended to or not. Since we are accustomed to being Pushed, it seems normal to be Pushed or managed as employees in business. Isn't that why we get paid?

Our past history causes us to have various degrees of fear about trying new possibilities, lest we fail in our attempt and have to be corrected. Managing in business today is often complicated by this history, so managers must learn how to manage human behaviors as well as finances.

Good managers are good at reading non-verbal signs and listening for what is driving individuals. They recognize Pull. It's no wonder that really effective business leaders are so rare.

Introducing Pull Thinking and Pull environments can be threatening to both employees and management. Anything new, no matter how positive, can be disturbing, simply because it threatens the status quo. There is a likelihood of activating others' fear of the unknown, since roles, behaviors and responsibilities—as well as measures of success—will change. People fear they'll have to learn where the "hot pots" are all over again.

Likewise, trying to follow a recipe on the technical aspects of implementing a Pull environment without an understanding of how Pull Thinking works will also be uncomfortable. Imagine putting together a model kit with no instructions and no picture on the box.

Experience has shown that Pull Thinking works much better when one understands why and how it works and can resonate with the process and the possibilities.

Defining service

Serving the customer will become the highest purpose that will be used to align everyone and every action in the organization. A definition of service used in Pull Thinking is: "work performed for others. We grow through providing service.

In the examples below, who is Fred serving? Let's take a look.

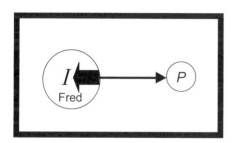 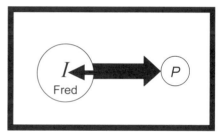

In the drawing on the left, the Pull of the *I* (Fred's identity) is greater than the pull of *P*, so Fred is staying inside himself. Since there is little or no work or energy flowing from him to *P*, there is little or no service being performed. Quality of service is poor and costly. Customer complaints are high. Dissonance is loud.

In the right drawing, Fred is going outside of himself to perform work for *P*—this is serving the Project's purpose. Quality of service is high, costs are low, complaints are rare, and resonance is high.

Only through service is there the opportunity to enhance our service identity. That part of our identity contains what we know about service — the images, assumptions and measures regarding service — our service mental model. Just as we must exercise a muscle for it to grow stronger, we must practice service to strengthen our service identity. This is true for individuals, teams, business units, and businesses across supply chains.

> *"I don't know what your destiny will be, but one thing I know; the only ones among you who will be really happy are those who will have sought and found how to serve."*
> Dr. Albert Schweitzer
> 1931

Seeing our identity as containing many mental models helps us understand what causes resistance to growth from the Pull of great ideas. Wanting to remove the resistance is part of the process of reducing the dissonance in achieving Ultimate Service resonance. In his book *The Fifth Discipline*, Peter Senge talks about the importance of understanding mental models when building learning organizations.

Why The Best Ideas Fail

"One thing all managers know is that many of the best ideas never get put into practice. Brilliant strategies fail to get translated into action. Systemic insights never find their way into operation policies. A pilot experiment may prove to everyone's satisfaction that a new approach leads to better results, but widespread adoption of the approach never occurs.

We are coming increasingly to believe that this "slip 'twixt cup and lip" stems, not from weak intentions, wavering will, or even non-systemic understanding, but from mental models. More specifically, new insights fail to get put into practice because they conflict with deeply held internal images of how the world works, images that limit us to familiar ways of thinking and acting. That is why the discipline of managing mental models – surfacing, testing, and improving our internal pictures of how the world works – promises to be a major breakthrough for building learning organizations."[2]

Service in business versus service in non-business activities

Everyone has constant opportunities to give service to customers. However, not all of these service opportunities are considered business activities.

For example, as a parent, you constantly give service to your children (your customers) by feeding, clothing, housing, carpooling, entertaining, and caring for them. As part of the parenting process, you grow through your service to them. Your acknowledgments come in forms other than money.

Another example of service in a non-business activity is a law firm doing "pro-bono" work for an indigent client. In this case, the law firm is performing service to a client and to society by providing their services at no charge. What does the law firm get as their acknowledgement? Satisfaction of protecting the innocent, experience in high profile cases, prestige for the law firm, a better society, and other "intangible" rewards like these.

In contrast, in business activities, service given to a customer will be acknowledged by money.

The important point is that in either business or non-business activities, the purpose of the activity is service, not acknowledgement through money or rewards. From an Ultimate Service point of view, integrity means the focus must be on the organization providing service to your customers—if that is what you say your business is about. "Walk the talk."

Where does money come in?

Since you're probably wondering about money, as it's a big concern and the lifeblood of business (a Pull), let's briefly put it into

---

[2] Peter M. Senge, *The Fifth Discipline*, page 174, Currency Doubleday, 1990

the Pull perspective. It will be discussed in more detail in Steps 3, 4, and 7.

What part does money play in Pull? In Pull Thinking, *money is an acknowledgment of success and of excellent service received.*

If the primary purpose of your business is to make money, you are not aligned with the customer. Your customer wants excellent service and is not concerned with your profits. Instead, money *supports* the business and must be Pulled in at the bottom of a Service Flow Pull Structure as an acknowledgement of service received. Businesses are usually in it for the money first. That's a formula for something less than the best possible service, and a clumsy process at best. The customer is left to choose the business that is the least clumsy.

"...service to humanity is the best work of life."
— From the Jaycee Creed

How service makes us happy

To support Ultimate Service growth, it is important to understand what is pulling people's behaviors. Since our measures and values form the boundaries of our behaviors, the logic is pretty simple:

- Success is when we are happy
- We are happy when we grow
- We grow through service
- We are happy giving service

Is there ultimate happiness in Ultimate Service?

Aren't we all attracted to being happy as often as possible? We all want to feel good; we are built that way. Therefore, since most of us are happy when we serve others and are happy to learn new things, is it not inherently obvious that we are attracted to growth?

To grow by learning how to better serve others could then be considered a double contribution towards happiness. The Pull of Ultimate Service produces ultimate growth and happiness.

Look at the alternative—feeling bad, being sad, or being bored with life. How could one be bored with learning, serving others, and growing? Isn't that really living?

Wouldn't it be great to be really living during work hours? Work hours make up *at least* a third of each day five days a week. And if you are bored at work, what are you doing after work?

Are you bored then, too?

Ultimate service in a Push environment

Ultimate Service will never be realized in a Push environment.

Think of it in terms as simple as "I have to be on time or my boss will yell at me" measured against, "I actually look forward to going to work in the mornings.

Yes, there will be individual and business growth, but it will be small compared to the growth possible in a Pull environment.

If choosing to be Pushed is the positive use of Push, then the negative side of Push is being Pushed without having requested it. Think of Fred—this time in a Push environment where he is being taken advantage of and treated poorly by his manager.

In the diagram on the following page, Fred's choice to stay in that environment must have a Pull, so obviously the "Pull of the *I*" is greater than the Pull of the possibility of things being better for him in a different environment.

By exploring the "Pull of the *I*," you can get at the root causes for Fred's lack of movement toward a Pull environment—typically fear of change or poor self-image.

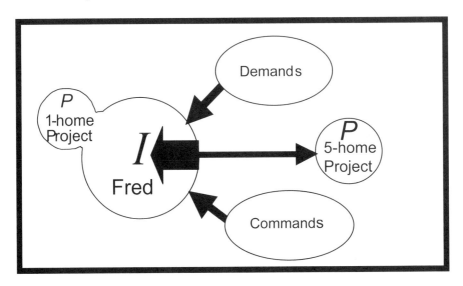

Pull affects other *I*s in your business

So far, we've been looking at the level of the individual. A business is made up of individuals, teams, business units, and groups, all trying to work together to produce products and deliver services for their customers.

How the individuals relate to each other and how the teams serve each other provide the structure of the business that serves the customers. In other words, the experiences employees have translate into the experiences customers have. That, of course, translates into the experience managers and shareholders have.

Everyone is linked. Each team or department has purposes that culminate in the common business purposes. Ideally, this all aligns with the customer's measures of success. If his needs have been met and he is satisfied with the outcome, the company is in the Pull of the customer. The customer will be loyal to the brand. Without a Pull, there is no service flow!

Each business has a service identity of its own. Growth of the individual *Service I* is the start of the growth of the team's *Service I*, which in turn contributes to the growth of the business's *Service I*.

The Pull of a possibility (*P*) attracts an individual to grow by giving service to others. The same concept applies to a team.

At the team level, when individuals come together, each choosing to be in the Pull of *P*, they create a new *Team Identity*. The team *Service I* represents the capabilities of the team to give service.

The drawing below shows Tom, Jim, Jane, and Sue as a team serving purpose P1. Over time purpose P1 is completed and everyone on the team grows.

The lower drawing illustrates the development of the team as a result of successfully accomplishing P1. They can then move on to the next purpose and, with the benefit of their experience, do an even better job with P2.

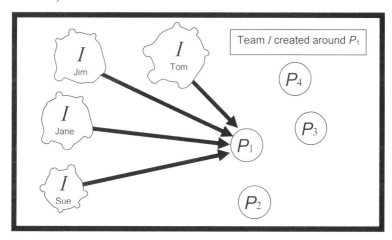

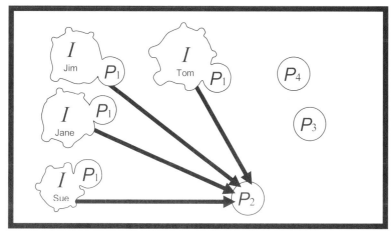

Growth occurs at all organizational levels

The diagram below shows the basic organization service flow. There are different service *I's* at each level. The service identities of various team and individuals make up the different levels of an organization. In each of the organization levels shown, the individuals are growing their *Service I*. As a result of their experience, the teams grow their *Service I*, and the business increases its *Service I*.

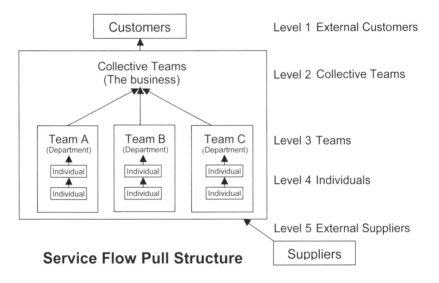

Service Flow Pull Structure

Converting service dissonance to service resonance

Dissonance exists all around us in various levels of service. It takes the form of poor employee attitudes, product quality problems, complaints, and added costs. Dissonance is never a positive thing.

In a dissonant environment, employees do not, on their own, consistently provide service that is in the Pull of the customers—internal or external. Managers are needed to get employees into alignment with the customer, because they can't or won't do so by themselves.

Employees working at 50 percent in the Pull of service equates to a need for twice as many employees and managers to achieve 100 percent service for the customer. This results in wasted time, lost revenue, and lower profits. And the employees working at 50 percent probably aren't happy, either. No one's winning here.

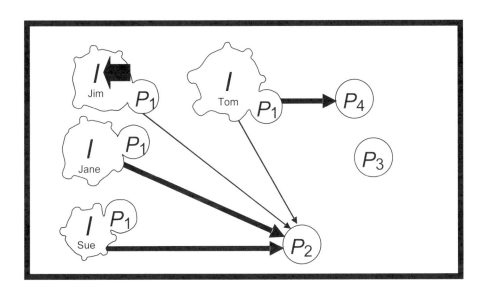

In the example above, the dissonance comes from Tom and Jim. They both have a weak Pull for P2. Jim is being Pulled more by some personal issues, and Tom has most of his attention on another project. The team has the effectiveness of two instead of four team members. The team is not "pulling together." There is some alignment but no resonance. They may appear to be a team but because of distractions of two of the team members, their resulting service actions will be cut almost in half.

In contrast, Ultimate Service is the highest possible service to the customer (either internal or external). When all employees are 100 percent in the Pull of the external customer, resonance is high and costs are low.

Since everyone in the Ultimate Service business is resonating with the customer and self-managed, managers are needed less and less. Instead, coaches and teachers can be utilized to enhance the growth of all of the employees.

The Ultimate Service process removes the barriers that limit our service possibilities at all levels. Suddenly, everyone in the organization is able to unite together in the Pull of the customer. With all efforts in support of the customer's Pull, the process of moving from dissonance to resonance begins. Service becomes more and more a "seemingly effortless" flow of energy.

Psychologist and author Mihaly Csikszentmihalyi writes in his book *Flow: The Psychology of Optimal Experience*:

> "It is for this reason that we called the optimal experience 'flow.' The short and simple word describes well the sense of seemingly effortless movement.
>
> The purpose of the flow is to keep on flowing, not looking for a peak or utopia but staying in the flow. It is not a moving up but a continuous flowing; you move up to keep the flow going. There is no possible reason for climbing itself; it is a self-communication."[3]

Home Depot, United Parcel Service, and Whole Foods are just a few examples of companies heading for Ultimate Service today. Many others can be found on the list of Fortune magazine's best 100 businesses to work for.

Csikszentmihalyi describes how culture produces flow in our thinking. The quote applies to any type of culture, including the business culture.

> "Cultures are defensive constructions against chaos, designed to reduce the impact of randomness on experience. They are adaptive responses, just as feathers are for birds and fur is for mammals. Cultures prescribe norms, evolve goals, and build beliefs that help us tackle the challenges of existence. In so doing they must rule out

---

[3] Csikszentmihalyi, Mihaly, *Flow, The Psychology of Optimal Experience,* Harper & Row, 1990

many alternative goals and beliefs, and thereby limit possibilities; but this channeling of attention to a limited set of goals and means is what allows effortless action within self-created boundaries."

The following two diagrams show illustrations that contrast two different companies, two different cultures, at both ends of the range of service capabilities.

In Typical Service Company X, there are two managers required to push the service through the employees to the customer. There are also rules, policies and directives rigidly in place to "keep the employees in line."

Typical Service - Company X

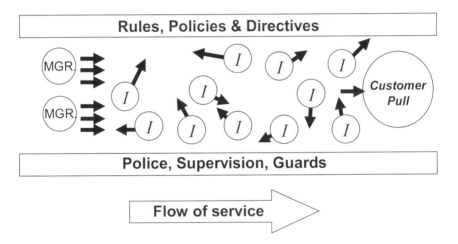

The flow of service is chaotic and unpredictable, because the employees' efforts are chaotic. Few employees (only the managers) are actually moving in the same direction. There are even employees moving in the <u>opposite</u> direction of the Pull of the Customer! Some employees are expending effort by bumping up against the rules, policies and directives of the company instead of serving the customer.

In the Typical Service Company X, there are many employees. Notice the small size of the *Service I* for these employees, compared to size of the *Service I* for the employees of the Ultimate Service Company Z shown in the following diagram. With this lack of alignment with the customer in Company X, what is the amount of service that is actually being given? What are the costs?

To improve the efficiency of the service, a company in a Push environment is going to reduce the width of the road and push even harder to get everyone going in the same direction. Pushing down the road is hard, full of pressure and delivers uncertain results. It is work — not fun!

What does Ultimate Service look like?

In contrast, Ultimate Service Company Z is able to serve the customer with fewer employees. No one is required to push the employees, because they are already in the Pull of the customer. There are no managers, because all employees are self-managed and trust has been established. While there are rules, policies, and directives, there is also more latitude for the employees to "move," while giving Ultimate Service, without undue restrictions. The costs are minimized!

Ultimate Service Company Z employees have a much bigger *Service I* than Typical Service Company X, and will therefore be more appealing to its external customers, since it can give better service. Company Z is also more attractive to prospective employees since it offers a much better work environment and supports their learning and growth.

Ultimate Service - Company Z

Rules, Policies & Directives

| I Supplier | → | I Customer / Supplier | → | I Customer / Supplier | → | Customer Pull |

Police, Supervision, Guards

Flow of service ▷

Pulling down the road is easy and orderly, and there's not much pressure. It is less like work and more like fun – action with less effort within self-created boundaries. This is the experience of "Flow," the result of Pull Thinking. This is what the Pull of Ultimate Service is all about. It's mental ergonomics.

> "As we abandon the machine imagery of the past, self-reference calls to me as the richest and most enticing teacher for how to be together in ways that support life, not destruction...It explains how life creates order without control, and stable identities that are open to change. It describes systems of relationships where both interdependence and individual autonomy are necessary conditions. It promises that as individuals together reference a chosen, shared identity, a coherent system can emerge. It illuminates the necessity for meaning-making in a world that often feels meaningless." Margaret J. Wheatley, *Leadership and the New Science*, ©1999, Pg. 168, Berrett-Koehler Publishers

In his famous novel *Treasure Island,* Robert Lewis Stevenson talked about lost gold before he introduced the pirate's map. After all, what good is a treasure map if you don't know there's gold at the end? What's the gold here?

From an Ultimate Service point of view, integrity means the focus is on the organization providing service to all customers. In an Ultimate Service environment, one enters every interaction seeking to provide better and more memorable service than the last time. It's not a static state, as needs and desires change and evolve over time. Ultimate Service (the gold) is a state of (Pulling for) continuous improvement—continuous growth.

Ultimate Service is hard to define, but you know it when you see it. Perhaps it's easier to define by its emotional consequence, or feeling.

Ultimate Service *feels* like:

- As a customer:
    - I'm being taken care of; there is no better service.
    - I am important, I can trust my supplier.
    - I am not imposing on anyone.
    - It is easy to communicate what I want because my needs are understood.
    - There is a consistent service experience from everyone in the organization.
    - Everyone is aligned toward service and listening for feedback.
    - Any complaint is easily remedied.
    - I could not have asked for any better service or product.
- As a supplier:
    - I am resonating with the customer. It's almost like knowing ahead of time what the customer's needs are.
    - I am confident and triumphant; it almost seems effortless.

Joy, elation, thrill, and memorable are words that describe various types of Ultimate Service experiences—both for the customer *and* the supplier. Wouldn't it be great to hear words like that more often? Or even all the time?

Ultimate Service is also about the values of suppliers, which can include:

- Honesty and trustworthiness
- Innovation and creativity
- Openness and flexibility
- Customer concern and passion
- Proactive service improvement

Ultimate Service is the experience of a "WOW" service impression. Each organization, team and individual needs to define what "WOW" service means for them. How? One hint: talk to your customers! Ask questions. They really *want* to give you feedback and they want you to succeed. Step 3 begins the process of putting the tools of Pull Thinking to work to help us understand how to Harness the Power of Pull beginning with the first of the Four Pull Questions — What is the purpose?

Step 3
The First Pull Question
People with Purpose

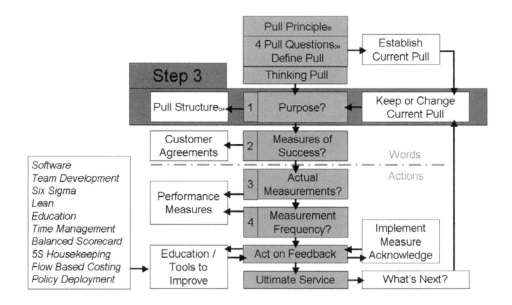

Pull Thinking Process

"In the absence of a Vision, we are each driven by our own agenda, finding people whose interests match ours, and inattentive to those with whom we appear to have little in common. We automatically judge our players, workers, and loved ones against our standards, inadvertently pulling the wind from their sails."

— Rosamund Stone Zander and Benjamin Zander,
The Art of Possibility

What is the purpose?

Purpose creates structure. Form follows function. Vision is a purpose statement. It answers the first of the Four Pull Questions. *Without a purpose, there is no Pull, and no reason to ask the other three Pull Questions.*

It's always critical to understand why we're doing what we do. Of course, there is no real power in a Vision by itself. The other three Pull Questions must also be answered. But it all starts with Vision. A company without a Vision will flounder, looking for things to do as the market evolves. It might even find a measure of success—for a while. Ultimately, it needs a Vision, a purpose— something that customers (remember, the term customer refers to your internal constituencies as well) can believe in and be loyal to.

The vision must cover the reason for being—the essential function of the organization, without which it loses its rationale for existing. An essential function is one that the organization exists to fulfill, as opposed to the functions it fulfills in order to exist.

Beginning in the 1980s, business paid increasing attention to Vision and Mission statements. As with any seemingly new idea, there was a jump on the bandwagon period. Years later, Visioning was seen as just another fad (like Management by Objectives or goal setting), and attention shifted to newer fads. Having a Vision statement in business is too often just one more thing to check off in order to be a respected business. Too often, the Vision or Mission statement was nothing more than empty words.

You know whether the Vision is powerful or not. It's at the top of the list of integrity checkpoints for any business. Is the Vision something that's good for all your customers? Does your team believe and embrace the Mission? Is it achievable? Is it worthwhile? Pull Thinking in practice starts with a Vision.

The importance of a Vision

Clearly, an overarching Vision is important to a business. A great Vision is as important for each department (like Accounting, Engineering, or Purchasing) as it is for project teams. What about the individual team members — shouldn't they have a Vision also?

The fact is, creating a great Vision is a skill most of us haven't developed well. Vision 101 isn't a part of the curriculum at most universities. That's understandable. After all, why should we develop a Vision? Isn't that always a top management thing? Besides, having our own team or personal Vision might make us seem like we're not behind the company's Vision. Unfortunately, that's not the kind of thinking that leads to Ultimate Service.

You've probably seen campaigns with Vision statements posted everywhere — in offices, hallways, and break rooms. Sometimes people read them, sometimes people don't. Sometimes people believe in them, sometimes people don't.

When they don't, something is wrong.

You may even have been lucky enough to really feel the power of a great Vision at work. That makes all the difference. A clear Vision, based on core values and beliefs, was the key to MindSpring's success in its early days. The fact is, an enterprise is likely to arrive where it wants to be if everyone knows where that is. They're more likely to succeed brilliantly if they all know what the company plans to achieve, and how their contributions help make the Vision real. That's not rocket science, but it's too often overlooked.

Everyone must, with complete integrity, be able to say that they understand, believe, and embrace the Vision. It must be a Pull. In Pull Thinking, Visions at all levels are shared among individuals, teams, customers, and company. Written communication provides visibility, thus enabling support.

"In a corporation, a shared Vision changes people's relationship with the company. It is no longer 'their company;' it becomes 'our company.' A shared Vision is the first step in allowing people who mistrusted each other to begin to work together. It creates a common identity. In fact, an organization's shared sense of purpose, Vision, and operation values establish the most basic level of commonality."
— Peter M. Senge, *The Fifth Discipline*

What is the difference between Vision, Mission, Goal, Objective, and Target?

To avoid confusion, it's important to first explore the meaning of these words in Pull Thinking and how they relate to purpose.

Everyone uses the words Vision, Mission, goal, objective, and target. The confusing part is that they are often interchanged, and that they have different meanings to different people. One thing they do have in common is that they are all statements of purpose.

Think of *Vision* as the highest purpose, with a broad, timeless description, enabling the most possibilities.

Mission is a short-term purpose, which is often a part of many other Missions, all aligned to accomplish a long-term purpose or Vision. Missions support the Vision in real-time, and refer to what actions will be taken within the next month, quarter or year. (Having a Mission lasting only a few hours or days could also be the case.) Vision and Mission are both purposes, each having their own measures of success. In a Vision statement, the measures of success and time are not explicitly articulated. But in a Mission they are.

You can think of Vision as a long range, high-level strategy and Mission as short range, lower level tactics, but that's oversimplifying a bit.

How a Vision is stated makes a big difference

Why should companies not include words referring to specific measures or time frame in a Vision statement?

In the 1960s, John F. Kennedy made a famous speech giving NASA a Mission: to land a man on the moon "by the end of this decade." Obviously, that was accomplished, and it was a pretty incredible achievement. But what's happened since? The space program—and the public's interest—waned without another Vision to excite the popular imagination.

Measures and time frames limit one's imagination. For example, if in 1942 we could have had a choice between these two Visions:

"Everyone in this city breathes smog free air in 2002"	vs.	"Everyone in this city breathes clean air"

Which one would have had the most effect during the subsequent 60 years?

By including the measure "smog free" in the first Vision, we are limiting our measures to visible smog. In 1942, science did not have the same measure on pollution that we have today (Particles/million). The electron microscope and other similar equipment did not exist then. Also, the time frame "2002" would not have a sustained urgency—if visible smog could have been eliminated by 1960, it would have stopped the quest for even cleaner air.

The second Vision leaves open the timeframe and the measure. The definition of "clean" changes when better measuring equipment becomes available, and the timeframe moves out. The second Vision lives forever into the future.

Who knows what the definition of clean air will be thirty years from now? Having minute impurities in the air may be considered acceptable now, due to present technology limitations. In thirty years, however, having a means to detect and remove these particles will redefine "clean-air" as air without these impurities. Under this Vision, there will always be motivation to act.

Here's another example of a limiting Vision:

"64K of memory is all anyone needs in their personal computer"	vs.	"Computers with ever-increasing memory"

Which Vision will endure? Which leads to greater success over time?

Formalizing definitions

Let's take a look at the dictionary definitions of the terms we're using in the context of Pull Thinking:

Vision
a) the ability to perceive something not actually visible, as through mental acuteness or keen foresight [a project made possible by one man's Vision] b) force or power of imagination [a statesman of great Vision]

Describing a Vision in words, both orally and in writing, helps to solidify the picture and provides the possibility for support. It also helps ensure that all have the same Vision (picture of the future) in mind. Thus many can participate in shaping strategies, decisions and actions needed to realize the power of the Vision.

Mission
a sending out or being sent out with authority to perform a special service

Missions are the most real-time expression of the Pull at work. Missions are often stated as "Our purpose is to..." in order to create the Vision.

If your Vision is unlimited knowledge of the universe, delight in diversity, and peaceful relations with all life, then your Mission might be to "explore strange new worlds and seek out new life and new civilizations." The Missions are steps that help the Vision become real. Vision should be eternal; Missions change and evolve. Visions are strategic; Missions are tactical.

Goal, Target
an object or end that one strives to attain; aim

These are just too weak for a Pull, unless the Goal is part of a Mission to achieve a Vision. There's just not enough "meat on the bone" to simply do goal setting, especially in the context of Pull Thinking. They're too short term. Goals and Targets can be effective as milestones along the journey (my goal is to finish this report by noon), but a Goal is limiting. Once the Goal is reached, the motivation ends. What happens *after* the report is finished at noon?

Objective
the aim or goal

Again, Objective is similar definition to goal or target. The best position for objectives is often used as a sub-goal in support of a Goal or Target.

> Vision – Purpose
>> Mission – Sub-Purpose
>>> Goal / Target – Sub-Sub-Purpose
>>> Objective – Sub-Sub-Sub-Purpose

How do you know when you have a good Vision or Mission statement?

Let's take a quick look at what some others have to say about Vision and Missions. The views here are intended to give you some other perspectives—to give you a good sample of how the leading thinkers on the subject of Vision and Missions. These might give you some ideas for further reading.

The book *The Art of Possibility* offers an excellent description of the attributes of a good Vision statement. Here are the criteria that enable a Vision to stand in the universe of possibility:

- A Vision articulates a possibility.
- A Vision fulfills a desire fundamental to humankind, a desire with which any human being can resonate. It is an idea to which no one could logically respond, "What about me?"
- A Vision makes no reference to morality or ethics; it is not about a right way of doing things. It cannot imply that anyone is wrong.

- A Vision is stated as a picture for all time, using no numbers, measures, or comparatives. It contains no specifics of time, place, audience, or product.
- A Vision is freestanding—it points neither to a rosier future, nor to a past in need of improvement. It gives over its bounty now. If the Mission is "peace on earth," peace comes with its utterance. When "the possibility of ideas making a difference" is spoken, at that moment ideas do make a difference.
- A Vision is a long line of possibility radiating outward. It invites infinite expression, development, and proliferation within its definitional framework.
- Speaking a Vision transforms the speaker. For that moment the "real world" becomes a universe of possibility and the barriers to the realization of the Vision disappear." [1]

Dr. Stephen R. Covey wrote these words on Vision:

> "Vision is the best manifestation of creative imagination and the primary motivation of human action. It's the ability to see beyond our present reality, to create, to invent what does not yet exist, to become what we are not yet. It gives us capacity to live out of our imagination instead of our memory."

A good Vision:
- Inspires and brings out passion
- Describes the future you see and are experiencing *now*
- Can easily be seen and related to by others
- Is reachable but still quite a stretch
- Is expressed in simple terms in as few words as possible
- Is easy to remember
- Is not an illusion
- Is not limited by time

---

[1] Rosamund Stone Zander & Benjamin Zander, *The Art of Possibility*, Harvard Business School Press, 2000

- Includes measures like highest, or best (but doesn't include financial or numerical measures)

A good Mission:
- Supports the Vision
- Defines measures of success easily
- Addresses balanced needs: financial, environmental, innovation, resources, and service relationships
- Empowers
- Is accomplished soon
- Describes a process
- Contains the words "to" or "to create...."
- Can include timing
- May include financial or numerical measures
- Doesn't contain words like "we will" or "we shall" or "we must" or "we should" or "we shall"

Understanding the power of Vision

> "The compelling nature of a Preferred Future image that people have created together forms a powerful basis for action. People support what they have been part of creating and begin immediately to act in ways that ensure they will achieve it. The Preferred Future comes about as a result of 'behaving our way into the future' and 'beginning with the end in mind.'" [2]

"Being of one brain and one heart is the alchemy of Whole-Scale Change."

— Dannemiller Tyson Associates

---

[2] Covey, Stephen R., *First Things First*, Fireside and Colophon, 1995

Peter Senge has a lot to say about Vision in his book *The Fifth Discipline*. This book is also an excellent resource for more ideas and understanding on how to develop a learning environment in business. Below are excerpts from Chapter 11:

On what a shared Vision is:

"Shared Vision is not an idea... It is, rather, a force in people's hearts, a force of impressive power.... If it is palpable, People begin to see it as if it exists."

"Shared Vision is vital for the learning organization because it provides the focus and energy for learning."

"A shared Vision, especially one that is intrinsic, uplifts people's aspirations. Work becomes part of pursuing a larger purpose embodied in the organizations' products or services."

On the process of creating shared and personal Vision:

"Organizations intent on building shared Visions continually encourage members to develop their personal Visions. If people don't have their own Vision, all they can do is 'sign up' for someone else's. The result is compliance, never commitment. On the other hand, people with a strong sense of personal direction can join together to create a powerful synergy toward what I/we truly want."

"Personal mastery is the bedrock for developing shared Visions."

"In encouraging personal Vision, organizations must be careful not to infringe on individual freedoms. ....no one can give another 'his Vision,' nor even force him to develop a Vision. However, there are positive actions that can be taken to create a positive climate that encourages personal Vision. The most direct is for leaders who have a sense of Vision to communicate that in such a way that others are encouraged to share their Visions. This is the art of Visionary leadership—how shared Visions are built from personal Visions."

"For those in leadership positions, what is most important is to remember that their Visions are still personal Visions. Just because they occupy a position of leadership does not mean that their personal Visions are *automatically* 'the organization's Vision.'"

"Today, it is common to hear managers talk of getting people to 'buy into' the Vision. For many, I fear, this suggests a sales process, where I sell and you buy. Yet, there is a world of difference between 'selling' and 'enrolling.' 'Selling' generally means getting someone to do something that he might not do if they were in full possession of all the facts. 'Enrolling,' by contrast, literally means 'placing one's name on the roll.' Enrollment implies free choice, while 'being sold' often does not."

In most contemporary organizations, there are relatively few people enrolled—and even fewer committed. The great majority of people are in a state of "compliance." "Compliant" followers go along with a Vision. They do what is expected of them. They support the Vision, to some degree. But, they are not truly enrolled or committed.

Compliance is often confused with enrollment and commitment. In part, this occurs because compliance has prevailed for so long in most organizations, we don't know how to recognize real commitment." [3]

To implement Pull Thinking, start with a powerful Vision

As you recall from Step One, Pull Thinking begins with understanding motivations—or Pull. Vision can—and should—be the ultimate Pull. A Vision must be something that people desire to

---

[3] Senge, Peter, *The Fifth Discipline* Currency Doubleday, 1990

accomplish. Vision begins with Pull. Why strive for cleaner air? Because cleaner air is a desirable outcome. It's a Pull.

One great thing about Pull Thinking is that it can start at any time, no matter what condition your business is in. It is never too late or too soon. But there's always the question about where to start first: with the structure, the Vision, or the Mission?

Pull Thinking requires that the first order of business be to start with the Vision. What's the primary pull? What do we want to accomplish? What does the customer want?

Dropping this down to the practical level, begin by taking a fresh look at the current Vision of the business to see if it is still a great inspiring Vision. If it's gone flat and is in need of refreshing, it's not a great Vision. If there is no Vision, it's time to create one.

Once that's accomplished, Mission statements need to be established for the overall business. Next, a basic Service Flow Pull Structure can be constructed showing all the Vision and Mission statements as links in a structure of customer/supplier service relationships.

Sometimes, subtle word choices can make a big difference. Here is an example of a fast-growing food supplier's Vision/Mission statement. The one on the left was posted everywhere in the company.

Notice the difference in the power of the Vision statement on the right after using Pull Thinking and refocusing more appropriately on the customer, and changing just a few words.

OUR VISION We will be the recognized leader in high quality, branded, fresh foods	**CUSTOMER VISION** Distinctive customer relationships that meet customer needs and exceed customer expectations
OUR MISSION Dominate the domestic retail grocery channel with high quality, branded fresh foods	**CUSTOMER MISSION** To create a variety of fresh salad experiences with unmatched taste, crispness, value and eye appeal that repeatedly delight our customers
OUR COMMITMENT A variety of fresh salad experiences with unmatched taste, crispness, value and eye appeal that repeatedly delight our customers	**OUR STOCKHOLDER VISION** Recognized leader in high quality, branded, fresh foods
OUR OBJECTIVE Distinctive customer relationships that meet customer needs and exceed customer expectations	**OUR STOCKHOLDER MISSION** To dominate the domestic retail grocery channel with high quality, branded fresh foods

The following are examples of actual Vision/Mission statements:

---

*Air*Tran® Airways

Vision

Innovative people dedicated to delivering the best flying experience to smart travelers. Every day.

Quest Worldwide

Vision

A global consultancy renowned for creating sustainable value by transforming performance and culture.

Great Vision statements

"Passionate music-making without boundaries"
- the Boston Philharmonic Orchestra

"The possibility of a world living in freedom"
- a group of U.S. Army officers

"The world pulling together"
- Alignment at Work, LLC

"The Ritz-Carlton experience enlivens the senses, instills well-being, and fulfills even the unexpressed wishes and needs of our guests."

"We serve the sweetest rewards"
- Cinnabon

Great Mission Statements

"At Baja Fresh® we strive to make our food fresh and hot, our restaurant clean, and our service friendly & efficient."

"To give each customer the assurance that their car is well-maintained by providing the highest quality automotive products and services delivered quickly and conveniently in a superior environment by a friendly, professional staff emphasizing integrity in every action.
- Express Oil Change

"Our mission is to encourage and develop creative leadership and effective management for the good of society overall."
- Center for Creative Leadership

Legal Department

MISSION

We will bring value to the Company by providing quality legal services taking into account the resources available to us.

We will support our clients and each other in their quest for success, meeting challenges in a proactive and effective manner in a time frame, which respects the priorities of all involved. We will provide legal support always with a healthy respect for the law, embracing constructive and ethical considerations, never to be dishonest or without dignity. We will always strive to improve our services, and we will listen constructively and respond to our clients' need using our full resources and imaginations.

The mission statement above could be improved. By making the first sentence the Mission statement and changing the second paragraph to be composed of measures of success regarding the Mission statement, we bring clarity on what needs to be measured. For example:

Mission: To bring value to the Company by providing quality legal services.

Success is that we support our clients proactively and effectively.

Success is that we always have a healthy respect for the law.

Success is that we are always honest.

Success is that we always have dignity.

Success is that we listen constructively.

Success is that we respond to clients using full resources and imaginations.

(Measures of success will be covered in more detail in Step 4)

Who should be involved in creating Vision/Mission statements?

Since every supplier of service within a business (individual, team, department, and group) will be involved, they will all eventually need to answer the first of the Four Pull Questions: "What is our purpose?" or "What are our business purposes?" The purposes will first be described in terms of the 'Preferred Future', and then in terms of the present action to make the Vision real (via a Mission). The Vision would be a description of what Ultimate Service looks like in the eyes of the customer once achieved in the future.

The Mission describes the daily purpose regarding serving the customer. Whatever you decide to call the different types of purposes, in Pull Thinking they are all purposes that answer the first of the Four Pull Questions.

"All that we do is done with an eye toward something else."
— Aristotle

In Pull Thinking, the easy part is often creating the overall business's Vision followed by each team or department's Vision of purpose. For example:

Purchasing Team Vision:

"Linking the flow of goods and services with suppliers that deliver the finest and most economical products."

The difficulty is often in getting to the individual or personal Vision. How will individuals connect with the business's Vision? How will they support it? Education and training in Visioning is an important step in the process. The Service Flow Pull Structure shows the connections.

From the very beginning, all participants must have a clear understanding of Pull Thinking. This has been proven on teams from the hourly staff level to executive level. Quite simply, this makes Visioning much easier. It provides a real purpose (and motivation) for learning how to create a Vision, rather than Visioning to satisfy "yet another management dictate."

People can relate to Visioning as a natural thing to do in a Pull Thinking context. There's really nothing to lose and much to gain: more possibilities, self-control, learning, growth, and most important—MORE FUN!

A personal Vision makes employees feel more a part of an enterprise's direction and success. It makes them feel empowered. There's a reason for that. They are empowered.

But a Vision needs structure to move from the realm of the idea into the "real world." A great Vision *without structure* will just sit there, merely looking pretty—but without action or effect. A great Vision cries out for a structure to fulfill its possibilities and to link the future to the present. It makes the vision look possible.

The quote by Winston Churchill below points to the need for structure to support creating a Vision. Without structure, one risks looking too far ahead. How far into the future should we look? As far as your structure can connect you.

"It is a mistake to look too far ahead. Only one link of the chain of destiny can be grasped at a time."
—Winston Churchill

Generic Manufacturing Company, Inc.

Vision

We are a World Class manufacturing enterprise that is rewarding and fosters trust and stability for our customers, suppliers and employees.

Our customers are totally delighted with excellence in quality, service and price.

Our employees experience pride and personal growth thru team involvement, a secure and appreciative environment, and financial rewards.

Our suppliers are proud and valued team members that experience continuous growth, appreciation and financial rewards.

The above generic Vision statement example, although long, does address the organization as an enterprise composed of three main components: external customers, employees and suppliers. This illustrates how to represent the components of an enterprise with more than one vision. What is needed is a Pull Structure composed of many visions all aligned in support of the overall enterprise Vision.

How do we get a flow of service?

In an Ultimate Service Flow Pull Structure, there are many Visions and Missions. Each business level has them: from the collective team (or total business), down to each team, and ultimately to each team member. In other words, all internal and external suppliers of service have a Vision with Missions of support. For example, each person or team member has at least three Visions: personal Vision, team Vision, and business (collective team) Vision.

A Service Flow Pull Structure is a chain of purposes composed of links. For now, let's focus on purpose to create the structure. Eventually, each link will be composed of the Four Pull Questions:

1. What is the purpose?

4. What is the frequency with which the measurements are being taken?

2. What are the measures of success?

Q1

Q2

Q4

Q3

3. What is actually being measured?

Creating a Service Flow Pull Structure

The links connect, starting with the end customers at the top and progressing down, showing the customer/supplier positions. The idea is to represent the external customers at the top pulling as if lifting a weight. Customers are pulling the suppliers. Note that each internal customer (employee) is also a supplier.

In Pull Thinking, your Mission is "to serve your customer."

1. Identify your end customer (internal or external) at the top. That will be the upper link to which you ultimately connect. It answers the question: "Why?" Serving the customer is *always* the "why."

2. Identify your support (*How* am I going to get what I need? How does support happen? Who will supply the support needed?) That will be the lower link, your supplier, that attaches to you. What the company, team, or individual does to serve the customer is always the "how."

3. After the structure has been created, write the answers to the Four Pull Questions for each link.

4. When customer and supplier agree on the answers to the Four Pull Questions that link them, the Pull is defined – it is a Pull and the link is shown with a solid outline or solid color.

5. If there is not agreement on the answers to the Four Pull Questions that link them, the Pull is not defined – it is a Push and the link is shown with an incomplete outline or transparent link section as shown in the following diagram:

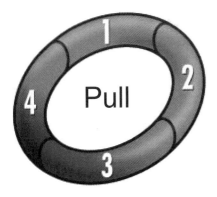

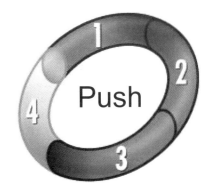

Strong Pull = Pull: all Four Pull Questions are answered and agreed upon between supplier and customer	Weak Pull = Push: when any one Pull Question (shown transparent) is not answered or not in agreement with both customer and supplier.

Each category of customer will have a unique structure to support their service flow. For each category of customer, draw a link for the name of the service provided. If one service is common to several categories of customers, draw one link and list the customers. The important objective is to show each different service in its own link. Later, we'll write the answers to the Four Pull Questions for each link as we progress through Steps 4, 5, and 6.

The diagram below shows a basic example of a Service Flow Pull Structure for a small business called Wood Products, Inc. In their business, they receive wood that is cut to their specifications from an outside supplier. They paint it, and then pack and ship it to their external customer.

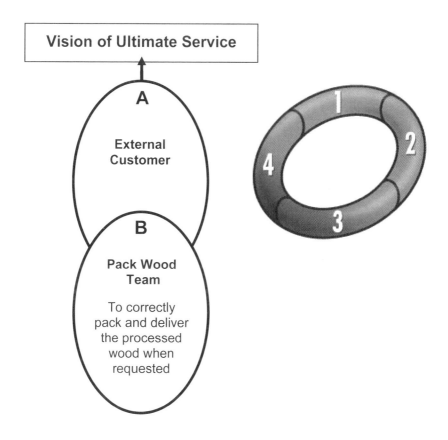

Now that the first links have been joined together, continue the process, and add the next supporting links:

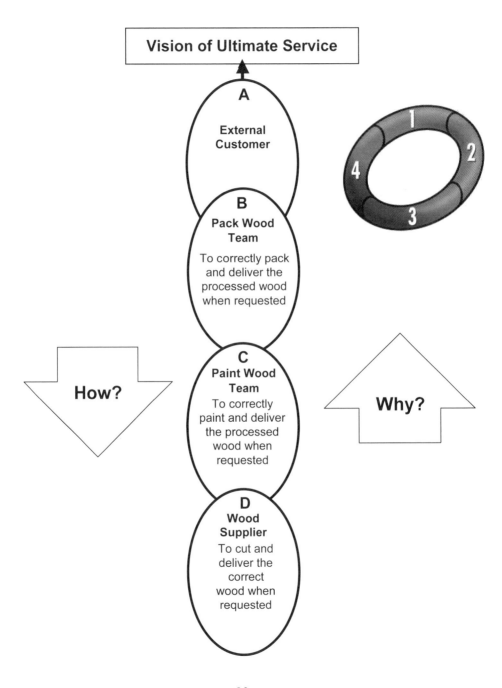

The diagram on the previous page shows the completed Service Flow Pull Structure. "What is the purpose?" Wood Product's teams B, C, and external Wood Supplier D are shown with the first of the Four Pull questions answered.

External supplier D's Pull comes from the Paint Wood team C. Team C's Pull comes from Pack Painted Wood Team B. Team B's Pull comes from the External Customer A.

Notice how the purposes build on each other. In each case, if you want to know "why," you follow the Service Flow Pull Structure UP. If you want to know "How," you follow the Service Flow Pull Structure DOWN.

The Service Flow Pull Structure can be created just from a Vision. Making the Vision real will be addressed in detail in Steps 4, 5 and 6 by answering Pull Questions 2, 3, and 4.

Service Flow Pull Structure

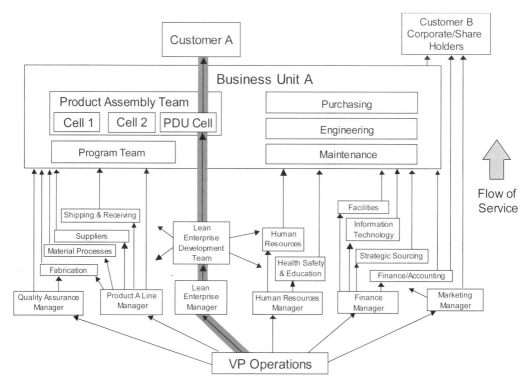

The diagram above is an example of a Service Flow Pull Structure developed for an aerospace manufacturing company:

Notice how it looks like an upside down organization chart. Arrows pointing to the internal and external customers help in the first steps of shifting thinking toward a focus on service.

This chart shows early on what Ultimate Service will look like. Of course, it may not really look like this in the end, but this gives everyone an idea of where the company is heading while being able to connect to the present organization chart.

An Ultimate Service pilot project was introduced as a learning tool for the rest of the organization. The gray line represents the first connections – the use of the pilot team – established in this company. The purpose for the pilot approach is to establish what one link of an

Ultimate Service Flow Pull Structure would look like for that business and serve as a learning tool for the rest of the business. Later in the book, examples will be presented showing each of the pilot project's completed Pull statements. This basic diagram below illustrates the structure of Pulls we want to achieve with each Pull having all of the Four Pull Questions answered.

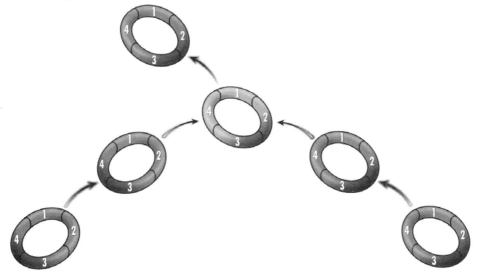

Service Flow Pull Structure

The following three diagrams show a generic soda business's Service Flow Pull Structure. The first diagram shows the overall business structure including supporting teams such as: Accounting, Quality Assurance, Administration Services and the Executive team. The second diagram shows only the basic core of the business structure. The third diagram represents one of the internal core teams, the Create Bottles of generic soda team. It is in this third diagram that we begin to see the individual people who actually make up the team and their supporting teams.

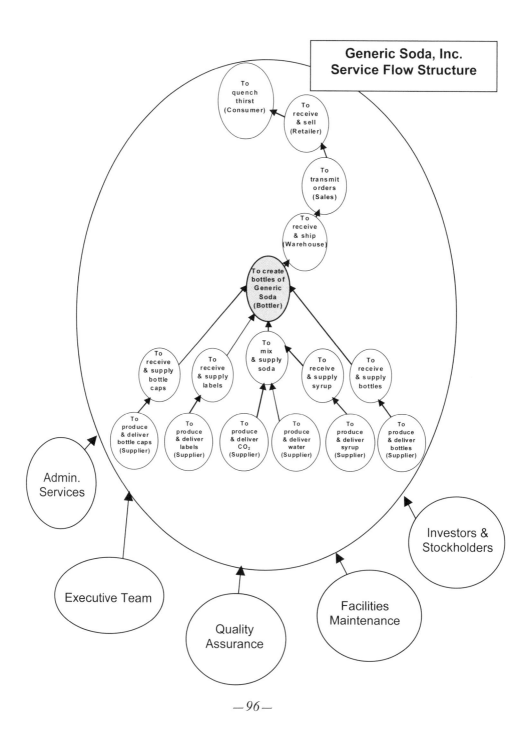

Generic Soda, Inc.
Service Flow Structure

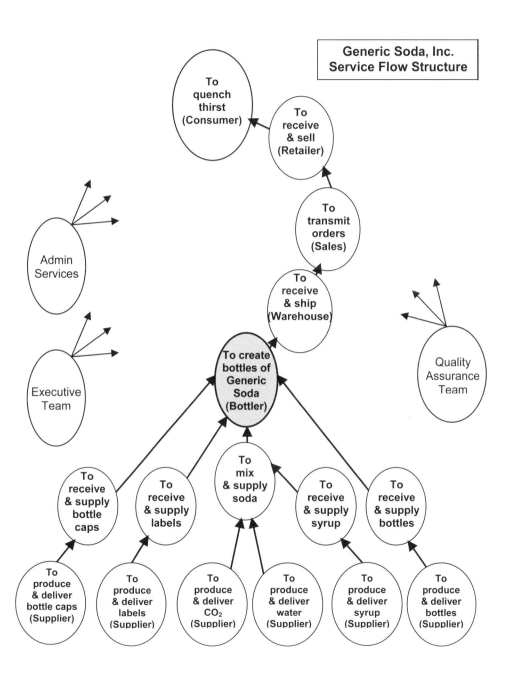

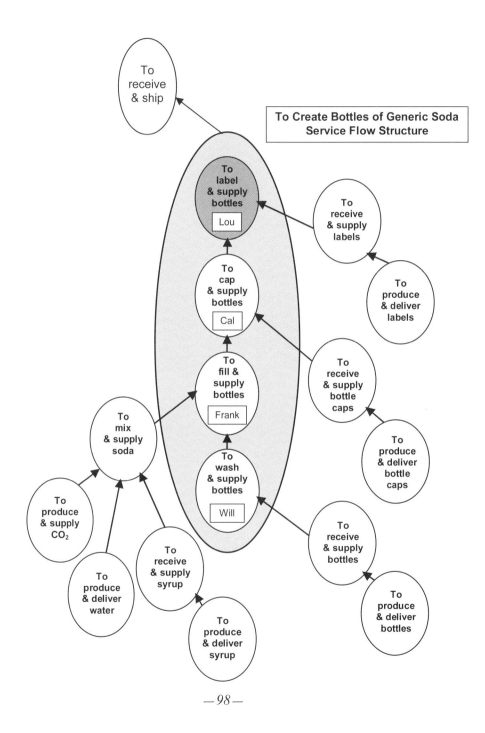

To Create Bottles of Generic Soda
Service Flow Structure

At this level, it's easy to see how the individual team members need their own purpose – mission – statement. Once the purpose is known, and the true customer is identified, each team, department, and individual can begin to establish the answer to the question: What does Ultimate Service look like for my customer? How do you get this information? You can guess, *or you can simply ask your customers!* In fact, agreement needs to be achieved between you and your customer on each of the Four Pull questions. This is discussed in detail in Step 4.

Process flow vs. service flow

Before leaving the last example, it is important to note the difference between a process flow and a service flow. A process flow shows first this purpose then that purpose – the sequence of events. Service flow may or may not be the same. The next purpose in a sequence is not necessarily the customer. In the above example, the three purposes: supplying water, CO2 and syrup each have "To mix and supply soda" as their customer, but the process may be: 1) Add water; 2) Mix in CO2; 3) Mix in syrup. In the example below, Marketing, Sales and Service Delivery are each a supplier to the external customer but the process sequence is: 1) Marketing; 2) Sales; 3) Service Delivery. Doing both a process and a Service Flow Pull Structure ties service to process. Without both, organizational alignment is difficult.

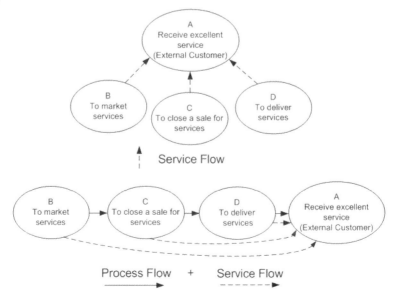

Culture and change in your business

Let's talk about your business culture today. That will change. One of the major changes relates to the primary purpose of the business. This change in business culture establishes *service* as the primary purpose of the business (even if your service is supplying a product). *Profit* is moved from the Vision/Mission purpose links, to links that refer to Accounting and Administration services links. These are the links that provide "Fuel" to support resources that are needed to create the Vision. (Step 4 details this.)

What is culture?

For our discussions, culture is defined as the collective measures of success or values shared by a group of people as a basis for making their day-to-day decisions. The culture of any business by this definition is really the sum of all of the measures of success of each individual regarding how they perform their work.

Therefore: A change in measure brings change in culture.

Since culture creates organizations, changing an organization begins with changing the culture. Remember the two measures from Step 1: The Four Pull Questions and the Pull Structure Service Flow Index. These two measures in Pull Thinking operate at the most fundamental cultural level and work to evolve the organization toward Ultimate Service Flow. Other measures such as financial are still important but appear in a different context and point in the structure.

Look at a business as being similar to a living organism, complete with individual cells. This is known as general systems theory. Each individual employee is compared to individual cells in this living organism. In a living organism, each cell is programmed according to the DNA of the organism. Likewise, from a Pull Thinking viewpoint, each individual employee of a business makes up the DNA in a chain of measures of success for that business. This analogy explains how Pull Thinking changes the business culture. In a living organism, the DNA structure supports the flow of energy or communication that creates, protects, and sustains the organism.

The same structure is needed for a business. For existing businesses, the structure supported its creation and is sustaining and maintaining the business at present.

It is more important to know how to change the future DNA structure than understand how the present DNA structure got this way. The structure must be an Ultimate Service Flow Pull Structure. It is *most* important to know how the present forces relate (or don't relate) to a Pull force within the Service Flow Pull Structure. Implementing a Service Flow Pull Structure is a culture change.

How to involve everyone in culture change

There are certainly many other ways of going about involving everyone in change, but one of the best comes from Dannemiller Tyson Associates. Change is best effected using representative cross-sections of groups to form "microcosms."[4].

A microcosm is a small representative system having analogies to a larger system in constitution, configuration, or development. Dannemiller Tyson writes:

> If you want to shift the whole system at one time, you must be able to think the way the whole system thinks. Using microcosms—real subsets of the larger group that represent all the "voices" of the organization—in the overall change process is one of the features of the Whole-Scale approach that allows you—and the organization—to think and see "whole system." The microcosm contains the essential "DNA" of the whole organization. Working with groups that mirror the "whole" allows you to work with the "whole system" at a different level. The best way to change a system is to engage the whole system. Microcosms are the best windows through which to view the whole system in real

---

[4] Dannemiller Tyson Associates, *Whole-Scale Change: Unleashing the Power of the Microcosm*, Berrett-Koehler Publishers, Inc., 2000

time. They provide access to the whole system quickly and effectively. Having a critical mass of microcosms experiencing a paradigm shift helps the whole organization shift.

Success is in all the people of the organization. The most effective change efforts include the voices of all key stakeholders, not just the voices of the top or the bottom or the middle. All of the people in the organization— plus those who are counting on the organization, such as customers, owners, or suppliers—must be able to speak and be heard. When you cannot get all— getting the "DNA" re-creates the whole, without having to have everyone. The decisions of any one representative microcosm should be exactly the same as those of any other "DNA" microcosm would be.

Of course, without an Ultimate Service Flow Pull Structure in place, there can be no flow of Ultimate Service. It would be like taking a section of pipe out of your plumbing system—the flow of water would never reach the sink. Your business has a flow of service now, but is it the structure working to support the flow of Ultimate Service? Your pipes may be clogged with the scale of misaligned purposes. Or it might be that the size of your pipes or the design of your plumbing system restricts or diverts the flow, increasing the pressure on the whole system.

The Ultimate Service Flow Pull Structure to be defined resonates a clear flow of communication between internal and external suppliers and customers, and creates Ultimate Service. Using the language of Pull Thinking provides the basis for the most efficient method of communication possible. The pipes are clean and smooth. The system is designed to allow maximum flow.

There is a great discussion regarding purpose, flow and structure in *Chaos—the Making of a New Science* by James Gleick. It brings more understanding to the importance of structure with regards to purpose and flow from a scientific point of view:

> Nature forms patterns. Some are orderly in space but disorderly in time, others orderly in time but disorderly

in space. Some patterns are fractal, exhibiting structures self-similar in scale.

The heart of the new snowflake model is the essence of chaos: a delicate balance between forces of stability and forces of instability; a powerful interplay of forces on atomic scales and forces on everyday scales.

Theodore Schwend, a Swiss philosopher, believed in universal principles. His "archetypal principle" was this: "flow wants to realize itself, regardless of the surrounding material."

This can apply to the structure of the business organization.

Final cause is cause based on purpose or design: a wheel is round because that shape makes transportation possible. Physical cause is mechanical: the earth is round because gravity Pulls a spinning fluid into a spheroid. The distinction is not always so obvious. A drinking glass is round because that is the most comfortable shape to hold or drink from. A drinking glass is round because that is the shape naturally assumed by spun pottery or blown glass.

D'Arcy Thompson (a great biologist) wrote, "Natural selection operates not on genes or embryos, but on the final product. So an adaptionist explanation for the shape of an organism or the function of an organ always looks to its cause, not its physical cause but its final cause.[5]

In business, the "final cause" would be its ultimate purpose or Vision. The "universal principles" referred to here say: "Flow wants to realize itself." This idea supports the essence of the Pull Principle and Pull Thinking.

---

[5] Gleick, James, *Chaos — The Making of a New Science*, Penguin Books, 1987

Your Service Flow Pull Structure should support the Ultimate Service that is already inside each of us wanting to come out, where our passion for performance exists. If Ultimate Service is looking to realize itself, why not find the structure that lets that happen? Once you have your Service Flow Pull Structure designed, implementing it becomes your strategic process.

"Thus the invisible forces are ever working for a man who is always 'Pulling the strings' himself, though he does not know it. Owing to the vibratory power of words, whatever man voices, he begins to attract."
— Florence Scovel Shinn, *The Game of Life*

The quote above says a lot about the power of words and the value of putting "Pull" into words. Having a clear Vision/Mission with a supporting Service Flow Pull Structure and measures are crucial, as they serve to always keep our purpose forward in our thinking.

Margaret Wheatley wrote this regarding identity self reference:[6]

Companies organized around a strong identity provide a good example of how self-reference works to create greater stability and autonomy. When an organization knows who it is, what its strengths are, and what it is trying to accomplish, it can respond intelligently to changes from its environment. What ever it decides to do is determined by this clear sense of self, not just because a new trend or market has appeared. The organization does not get locked into supporting certain products or business units just because they exist, or following after every fad just because it shows up. The presence of a clear identity makes the organization less vulnerable to its environment; it develops greater freedom to decide how it will respond.

---

[6] Wheatley, Margaret J., *Leadership and the New Science*, Barrett-Koehler Publishers, 1999

Our "Preferred Future"

The probability of winning the lottery is zero if you don't buy a ticket. The probability of one getting aligned to a Vision/Mission when they don't exist or aren't communicated is also zero! You've got to buy a ticket. More, the odds of winning are *much* higher with a compelling Vision and supporting Missions.

There is high probability, however, that a Vision or Mission of getting paid is in our thoughts. That's not a bad thing, unless it's the biggest thing in our thinking, our primary motivation. If it is, it will cause a loss of focus on service. This loss of focus creates misalignment with the customer and leaves them with service that needs to be managed and "pushed."

Build it in our minds and it will become!

We can create our own reality, and we can buy our own Vision/Mission ticket. The values and measures upon which we choose to act upon are windows into the actual Vision/Mission at work. Steps 4, 5, and 6 discuss in detail the various aspects of valuing and measuring that bring reality to visions and missions.

Step 4
The Second Pull Question
Define Measures of Success

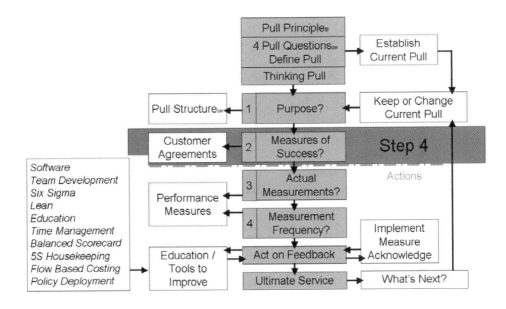

Pull Thinking Process

"The hypothesis has been proposed that if the mind of Man is exposed to the economy of Nature, as revealed in the workings of living systems, he will become sensitized to recognize the necessity of balancing values. Thus measure is established as the source of wisdom."
— Dr. Jonas Salk, *The Survival of the Wisest*

What are the Measures of Success?

We've all accumulated measures over the years. We all learn new measures (values and standards, for example) through education and experience in getting along with many different types of people. The older we are, the more wisdom potential we have. The amount of wisdom we gain is dependent on whether or not we apply the measures we know to useful purposes. We all want to be wise in order to accomplish, to create, and to be successful.

What are the Measures of Success? Having a Vision together with Measures of Success makes the Vision picture clearer for everyone. How do you determine the Measures of Success? As you see the Vision in your mind, begin to look for them. Even better, ask your customers! Share with them what you think and ask what they think success is, what Ultimate Service would look like to them. Ask them to rank the measures in order of importance. Once you have them, check them against your Vision/Mission statements. Do they line up with what is being said? If not, together with your customer, rewrite the Vision or Mission statement.

Often the Vision statement contains some of the Measures of Success in its wording. For example, take this Vision for a food service business:

"Creative people dedicated to providing the best dining experience to health-conscious guests, every day."

From this statement, the Measures of Success would be:

Hire "creative" people
Hire "dedicated" people
Deliver the "best" dining experience
Have "health conscious" guests

The answer to the third Pull question (What is actually being measured?) could easily be adapted. For example:

How creative? a scale of <u>Very</u> (creative) to <u>Unimaginative</u>
How dedicated? a scale of <u>Very</u> (dedicated) to <u>Disinterested</u>
Dining experience? a scale of <u>Best</u> (experience) to <u>Poor</u>
(experience).
What Kind of guest? a scale of 1 to 5 with 5 being <u>Health Conscious</u>
<u>Guests</u> and 1 being <u>Not Health Conscious Guests</u>.

Even the answer to the Fourth Pull Question (how often do we do this?) can be found: "Every day." This business wants to measure this <u>every day</u>!

What is a good Measure of Success?

This brings up another question. Does the Measure of Success statement contain enough information to enable you to determine the answers to Pull Questions Three and Four? We'll cover this in more detail in Steps Five and Six. Keeping this in mind will help you create a good Measure of Success statement the first time.

Looking at the Measures of Success above, one could then improve them by adding "very" to the first two bullet measures. Doing that completes the statement for all to see and leaves little chance for misinterpretation. Those responsible for being dedicated, for example, now know that the Measure of Success is "very dedicated" and not just "dedicated."

Original Vision		**Improved Vision**
"Creative people dedicated to providing the best dining experience to health conscious guests, everyday"	vs.	"Very creative people very dedicated to providing the best dining experience to health conscious guests, everyday"

Does being creative and dedicated mean the same as being very creative and very dedicated? What about extremely creative and extremely dedicated? Perhaps another business could have that as part of their Vision, thus raising the bar in the eyes of their customers.

Feedback must have a standard to measure success. By asking questions, we are often able to find out what measure was being used. To be successful, we need to know by what standard we are being measured.

When we don't know the standard for success, we become frustrated because we have to find it in a trial and error process. This is a classic Push, because all the answers to the Four Pull Questions are not known.

The measure in Push is commonly "not to make an error." If you *do* make an error (and most often only then), you'll be corrected. That is, unfortunately, how many of us were educated over the years. It doesn't feel good. When you don't know how to measure your performance, you need to be managed. Someone has to be there to correct you. If you have the measures, you don't need a manager.

Often people hesitate to complain for fear of reprisal. Recently, a neighbor considered registering a complaint with the postal letter carrier. Because the carrier was not closing the mailbox, the mail would get wet on rainy days. Others in the neighborhood advised him to be careful because they had received even worse service after complaining (especially to delivery supervisors). This kind of problem often results from a lack of competition.

The point is that measurement needs to be welcomed as an opportunity to improve – to come closer to the goal of Ultimate Service. More, the customer needs to feel welcomed and encouraged to provide measurement. The customer and the provider *both* need to feel a Pull to engage in measurement (feedback) and continual improvement.

It is possible to create Measures of Success by working with your customers on a trial and error process. For example, Jane has an administrative assistant, Bill, who seems to be away from his desk too often. She has complained to Bill often, but Bill doesn't know exactly what Jane wants. Out of frustration, Jane and Bill sit down and talk about it. They agree to have Bill carry a pager. That way when Jane needs Bill she can page him if he is away from his desk.

At the end of the day they meet and review how the day went. Jane, the customer, tells Bill, the supplier, the level of service she experienced. The first day Jane said that Bill's service was poor. It turned out that nine out of ten times, Bill was not at his desk. Jane had to page him. Excellence was then established as Bill being available ten out of ten times. Average would be five out of ten, or 50 percent of the time. Bill now has a clear understanding of what the scale of poor to excellent service means regarding being available when needed.

The Measure of Success is: *Success is being available 100 percent of the time*. The answer to Pull Question Three: "What is the actual measurement?" is *percentage of time available*.

After five days of experience, Bill puts the pager away and works to give excellent service. Part of the agreement between Bill and Jane was that it was okay for Bill to be away from his desk occasionally, but to let Jane know where he can be reached if needed. Bill was happy and Jane was happy.

Next, they needed to answer to the fourth Pull question: "What is the frequency?" They agreed to meet once a week to review and measure Jane's experience with Bill's service. After four weeks, Bill and Jane were satisfied that excellent service was being achieved and decided to change the frequency of measurement to once every three months.

Any kind of service measures can be established this way, provided, of course, that both customer and supplier agree and communicate well.

You may have heard the statement: "What gets measured gets done!" or: "If it's worth doing, it is worth measuring." The flip side to that is: "Whatever you're doing, measurement occurs whether you're conscious of it or not." The key is to bring the unconscious measurement forward in our thinking. Without the visibility of measures, we're left to wonder what we did to be so successful—or unsuccessful.

If one values something, there must be a reason and a resulting action. One takes measures to accomplish something. The Pull inherent in all of us is to give, to contribute and to improve upon a certain standard. A good example comes from Benjamin Zander, the conductor of the Boston Philharmonic Orchestra. On the first day of music class, his students are given a blank sheet of paper and asked to write down their Vision of why they received an "A" at the end of their course. Zander put it this way:

"The practice of giving the 'A' both invents and recognizes a universal desire in people to contribute to others, no matter how many barriers there are to its expression. We can choose to validate the apathy of a boss, a player, or a high school student and become resigned ourselves, or we can choose to honor in them an unfulfilled yearning to make a difference." [1]

The frequency of measure also plays an important role in the Measures of Success statement. The more frequent, intense, and passionate the measure, the higher the probability of success. When you keep the Vision in mind, the Measures of Success fall into place easily. If you're not used to thinking this way, however, Measures of

---

[1] Zander, Rosamond Stone and Benjamin, *The Art of the Possibility*, Harvard Business School Press, 2000

Success may seem unnatural. If it feels uncomfortable, it may be that the Vision is in need of more refinement.

Simply defining the Measures of Success will often bring about alignment where none existed before. Ultimate Service Measures of Success establish a visable bridge between the present and the future depicted in the Vision of Ultimate Service. This creates passion in the present, because knowing the Measures of Success ensures possibility. Without measures, there is only trial and error, and hoping that one's efforts are contributing to the overall purpose. You'll find more detail about passion and frequency in Step 6.

Attributes of a powerful Measure of Success statement:

- The actual measurement is stated or can easily be determined
- Objective rather than subjective
- Can be applied in terms of a unit of measure such as: percentage, scale (1 to 10 or poor to excellent, for example), feet, pounds, dollars, or miles per hour
- Easy to measure
- Customers and suppliers agree on the value of the measuremet
- More specific than general
- Applies to something you can do something about, and take action based on it
- Supports the Vision or Mission statement; brings clarity to the Vision/Mission
- The frequency of measurement is stated or can be easily determined
- The frequency of measurement is agreed upon by both customer and supplier

When formulating your Measures of Success statement, the key questions are:

- Who are your internal and external customers and suppliers?
- What are your Measures of Success
- Are they the same as the customers'?
- Do your customers really know their Measures of Success?

The following diagram shows a basic service flow from supplier to customer and supplier.

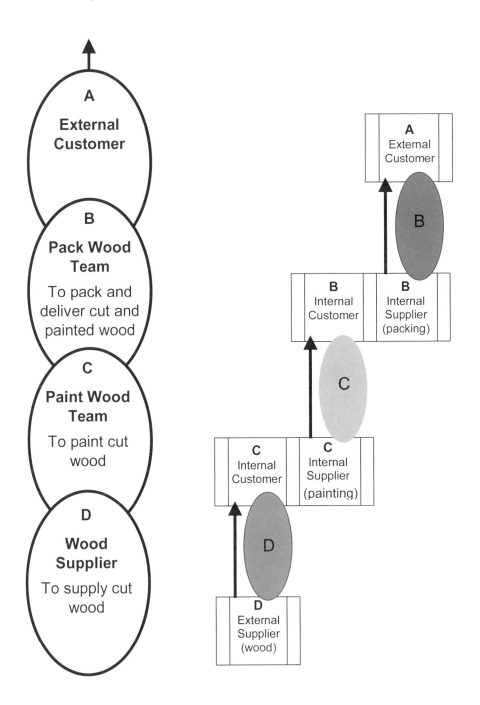

Internal customer C receives the purchased goods (wood plank) from external supplier D and provides service (paints it) to produce a painted wood plank. Internal customer C then becomes internal supplier C to provide painted wood planks to internal customer B. Internal customer B then packs the painted wood planks and supplies the final product to external customer A. The oval links represent Pulls, each answering the Four Pull Questions.

As was discussed in Step 1, the first two Pull Questions refer to the non-physical aspect of Pull. Question 1, "What is the purpose?", asks for the title or description of the Pull. That leaves all the rest of the information about a Pull to Question 2. The answer to Question 2 must therefore contain all the information needed to physically do the Pull. Questions 3 and 4 answers can be derived from reading the answers to Questions 1 and 2.

Why is this important? Integrity comes into play at this point. Form (or action) follows function. Questions 1 and 2 describe the function; questions 3 and 4 describe action or form. In order to communicate a function, we need to be able to say it. If the answers to questions 3 and 4 cannot be found in the answers to questions 1 and 2, there is no integrity. *Using these four questions puts a measure on integrity.* Integrity dictates that actions should be aligned with what was said. The phrase: "Do what you say and say what you do" applies here.

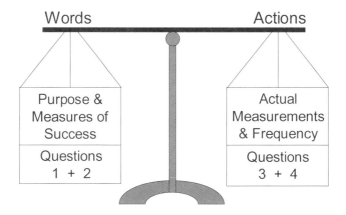

In the following diagram, the measure for B's Pull is: "loosely packed in a box" and the frequency is "2 days". The unit of measure is 'loosely' for "loosely packed". Not tightly, very tight or very loose, just loosely. The unit of measure for "in a box" would be 'yes or no'. The kind of box was not specified, but could be added later as an improvement.

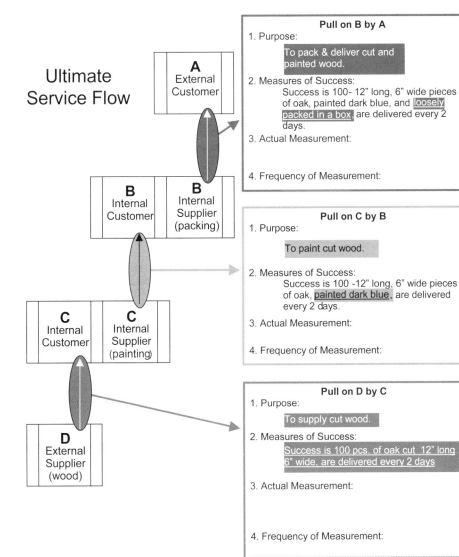

Pull on B by A
1. Purpose:
   To pack & deliver cut and painted wood.

2. Measures of Success:
   Success is 100- 12" long, 6" wide pieces of oak, painted dark blue, and loosely packed in a box, are delivered every 2 days.

3. Actual Measurement:

4. Frequency of Measurement:

Pull on C by B
1. Purpose:
   To paint cut wood.

2. Measures of Success:
   Success is 100 -12" long, 6" wide pieces of oak, painted dark blue, are delivered every 2 days.

3. Actual Measurement:

4. Frequency of Measurement:

Pull on D by C
1. Purpose:
   To supply cut wood.

2. Measures of Success:
   Success is 100 pcs. of oak cut 12" long 6" wide, are delivered every 2 days

3. Actual Measurement:

4. Frequency of Measurement:

Ultimate Service Flow

A
External Customer

B
Internal Customer

B
Internal Supplier (packing)

C
Internal Customer

C
Internal Supplier (painting)

D
External Supplier (wood)

It's important to make the Measures of Success appropriate to the purpose of the task at hand. Keep the measure and purpose on the same level of the Service Flow Pull Structure. Often the tendency is to connect a lower purpose measure to a higher purpose measure. Starting with the Service Flow Pull Structure helps prevent that. This tendency is illustrated in the following example where we will construct a service flow diagram for a software support team using only Pull Questions 1 and 2. Their job is to help users maximize their benefit from the software. They are the specialists that everyone in the company can call on for help.

> Their purpose is: To answer customer questions better.
> Success is: Team members receive over forty hours of training on product knowledge.

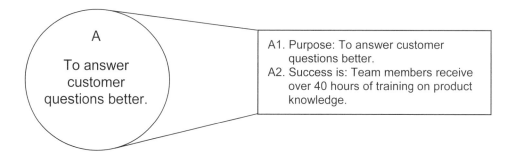

Measure of Success (A2) is misplaced in Service Flow Pull Structure

However, "40 hours of training" does not really measure how well customer questions are answered. Instead, it addresses "How" questions can be answered better. This is shown by adding a purpose link, "Increase team members' product knowledge" as purpose level B. Why? So team members can "answer customer questions better. "

The Measure of Success should be directly related to the purpose, in this case, "To answer customer questions better", such as, the "% of questions that are answered correctly raised from 50% to 95%."

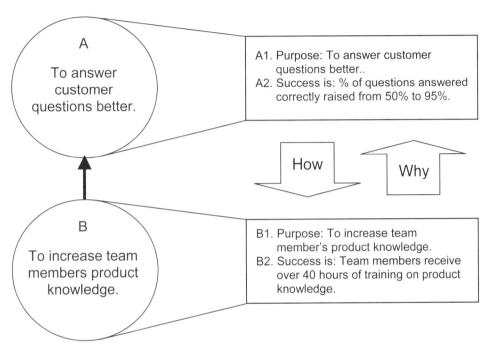

A

To answer customer questions better.

A1. Purpose: To answer customer questions better..
A2. Success is: % of questions answered correctly raised from 50% to 95%.

How   Why

B

To increase team members product knowledge.

B1. Purpose: To increase team member's product knowledge.
B2. Success is: Team members receive over 40 hours of training on product knowledge.

Measure of Success (B2) is again misplaced in Service Flow Pull

But there's still a problem.

Success regarding increasing team members' product knowledge is really better achieved with a direct measurement of team members' actual product knowledge. <u>How</u> to increase team members' knowledge would point to a lower level purpose, C, "To provide more team member training" as shown in the following diagram.

A

To answer customer questions better.

A1. Purpose: To answer customer questions better..
A2. Success is: % of questions answered correctly raised from 50% to 95%.

How   Why

B

To ensure team members know the product.

B1. Purpose: To ensure team members know the product..
B2. Success is: Team members pass product knowledge test with greater than 90%.

How   Why

C

To provide more team member training.

C1. Purpose: To provide more team member training.
C2. Success is: Team members receive over 40 hours product knowledge training.

Measures of Success are appropriately placed in the Service Flow Pull Structure

Note the Measures of Success and their position in the Service Flow Pull Structure. Why is that important? The issue here is one of focus and clarity. Not having the Measures of Success stated together with the correct purpose takes the focus away from the purpose, in this case, "Provide more training". Losing focus becomes a problem if you don't improve on answering customer questions when you provide more training. Why? Because you may tend to stop the program instead of looking for other possible ways ("How's") to support the A-level purpose of improving on correctly answered customer questions.

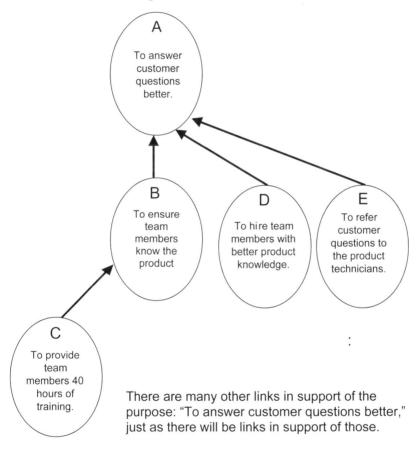

A
To answer customer questions better.

B
To ensure team members know the product

D
To hire team members with better product knowledge.

E
To refer customer questions to the product technicians.

C
To provide team members 40 hours of training.

There are many other links in support of the purpose: "To answer customer questions better," just as there will be links in support of those.

Given a clear focus on the primary purpose ("to answer customer questions better") and the Measure of Success ("to increase the percentage from 50 percent to 95 percent"), other "How's," (such as to test team members, to train team members, to hire team members with better product knowledge, or to refer customer questions to the product technicians) are more easily identified and engaged.

Staying focused on the primary purpose provides a higher probability of the team saying: "If providing forty hours of training to team members" does not improve the percentage of correctly answered customer questions, then what else can be done?"

This also is important in regard to responsibility. Since responsibility for improvement lies with the one doing the measuring (especially when others are involved) it's very important for the Measures of Success to be in the correct position in the Service Flow Pull Structure.

This diagram is another example showing one link of a Service Flow Pull Structure with misplaced Measures of Success. In this example, there are five Measures of Success (Pull Question 2) pulled by the purpose (Pull Question 1).

Company Y's purpose:
1. We are the preeminent (fill in the blank) service provider leading our industry through excellence, innovation, and growth.

2.1 Success is that our customers experience a very high degree of innovation in new kinds of services.
2.2 Success is that our customers experience excellence with all our services.
2.3 Success is that we have excellent growth each year.
2.4 Success is that we open 10 new stores each year.
2.5. Success is that our profits grow 10% each year.

Here's a simple way to see if Company Y's Measures of Success are properly placed in the Service Flow Pull Structure. Simply ask Company Y's customers what *their* Measures of Success are regarding company Y's purpose. Then see if they are the same as the 5 measures listed.

Measures 2.1, 2.2, and 2.3 probably are in line with external customer success measures regarding their service needs, while Measures of Success 2.4 and 2.5 probably are not. This is illustrated in the diagram below.

Measures 2.4 and 2.5 are really associated with other purposes that support company Y's stated purpose. These measures belong to the "How" question, and are purposes that support achieving the external customer's service needs. They must be properly placed in a lower part of the Service Flow Pull Structure, as shown in the following diagram.

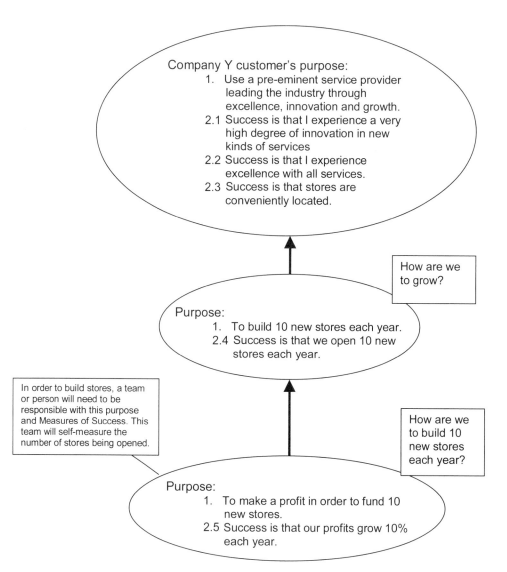

Company Y customer's purpose:
1. Use a pre-eminent service provider leading the industry through excellence, innovation and growth.
2.1 Success is that I experience a very high degree of innovation in new kinds of services
2.2 Success is that I experience excellence with all services.
2.3 Success is that stores are conveniently located.

How are we to grow?

Purpose:
1. To build 10 new stores each year.
2.4 Success is that we open 10 new stores each year.

In order to build stores, a team or person will need to be responsible with this purpose and Measures of Success. This team will self-measure the number of stores being opened.

How are we to build 10 new stores each year?

Purpose:
1. To make a profit in order to fund 10 new stores.
2.5 Success is that our profits grow 10% each year.

Another way to determine the Measure of Success is to ask, "Who is to provide the feedback?" or, "Who is the Customer for this purpose?" In this case, you certainly wouldn't ask your external customer if they experienced a 10 percent growth in profit or how many stores they opened last year.

In order to ensure profits, an Accounting Team or a designated individual is responsible for providing these Measures of Success, but not the actual profit growth. The Accounting Team provides measures regarding purposes that support "How" the profit growth will be created. The people who are actually responsible for accomplishing those purpose success measures (often the executives and managers) request the measurements from the Accounting Team.

Even though the Accounting Team performs the measurement, they are not responsible for taking actions to improve profits. The executives and managers are being held responsible for taking actions to achieve success. The Accounting Team simply provides the measurements by which the executives and managers are being held responsible.

So, in order to define Measures of Success in business, we can look to our customers (internal and external). Ask them to describe how they measure success and check to see if it matches with our own success measures. If they're different, it's time to align! However, customers aren't always clear about their own measures. If the customers aren't sure, ask questions about what you think their measures are. Ask, "What would Ultimate Service look like to you?" Getting agreement that your measures and the customer's are the same is crucial. Not doing so will leave open the possibility of getting a complaint when a missed service hits a hidden nerve.
Customers appreciate your wanting to get agreement on their measures. It communicates your sincere desire to provide Ultimate Service. Although often unintentional, most service problems are largely due to lack of agreement on both Measures of Success and frequency of measurement.

It is important to make the measures visible and share them with customers and employees to avoid misunderstandings. The "Visual Factory" common in manufacturing today is a very good method for doing this.

What would you think of an airline that had the courage to use Pull Thinking to improve their on-time performance? Could this really happen? Would it make a difference?

Red Airlines

Boarding Pass

Passengers must be at the gate 10 minutes prior to departure, or be denied boarding.

Green Airlines

Boarding Pass

Let's work together so we can leave on-time.

Please present yourself at the gate at least 20 minutes prior to departure.

Passengers must be at the gate 10 minutes prior to departure

Blue Airlines

Boarding Pass

Let's work together so we can leave on-time.

Please present yourself at the gate at least 20 minutes prior to departure.

Passengers must be at the gate 10 minutes prior to departure

On time goal: 95%

Yesterday's system-wide performance: 82%

How did we do?
Call: 1-800 Blue Air

Push

Pull Vision — better

Pull Vision and measures—best!

"A moment of truth is an episode in which a customer comes into contact with any aspect of the company, however remote, and thereby has an opportunity to form an impression."
—Jan Carlzon, President of SAS
Quoted in *Service America* by Karl Albrect and Ron Zemke

When customers and employees see that you are open with your service measures and results, they know you want to serve them better. Customers and employees are more apt to give honest feedback because they know it will be a win-win situation for everyone. We are not often accustomed to giving feedback this way. Instead, feedback is usually given when something goes wrong as we go down the road of trial and error. Being conscious of the measures allows everyone to be successful every day.

Tanya Chartrand, assistant professor of psychology at Ohio State University, describes studies showing the importance of understanding how success is measured. Researchers found that failing unconscious goals has negative effects on moods and performance. Conversely, she reports that succeeding at a goal you didn't know about has a positive effect on mood and performance[2]. Just think how much more positive it is to know the Measures of Success and know when and how you've succeeded. It would be a win-win for everyone, since the customer would also know that the process of improvement is in place.

Of course if there is no agreement on the measures, or success is not measurable, it may be time to stop. Trial and error may be the only way to proceed, but again, agreement between customer and supplier is crucial.

---

[2] Chartland, Tanya "Failure Has a Way of Getting You Down," *IE Soultions*, Sept. 2001, pg. 66

Who is responsible?

The person measuring or requesting the measure should be the person responsible and accountable.

The most efficient way to work is to let people and suppliers manage themselves, not to manage them. This is not news, but figuring out how to accomplish this is new and often challenging. Yes, employees may need to be managed during the transition, but only until their self-managing skills are developed. Then it's time to let go and let them grow their abilities.

Self-measures yield direct responsibility and thus indirect measures yield indirect responsibility. Which do you choose? In a Pull environment the CEO, COO, CFO, Director, and Manager, become teachers, mentors, and facilitators. They give the measures away to the staff to enable responsibility, self-measurement and empowerment.

Describing the measures with the Vision/Mission purpose statements brings alignment and clarity to the picture. Do the measures match the purpose? Are you measuring the right stuff? If you are, but the purpose doesn't match, it may be time to change the Vision/Mission or move the measures to the appropriate link.

When I went to renew my automobile registration at the county tag office, I asked an employee how she knew if she was being successful. She replied, "Because I just got a raise and my boss is happy." This employee's customers were people getting their auto registrations. She in fact was *not* helpful to anybody. She just did her job according to the book. Her raise was tied to the cost of living. Her boss was happy, because she always worked overtime when asked. Her customers, including myself, were not happy at all. We put up with poor service because we had nowhere else to go for these services. Later, to my delight, upon returning to renew my registration, I saw the following customer response form on the counter. I also found out that the employee was not working there anymore and there was a new county tax commissioner.

TOM SCOTT

DeKalb County Tax Commissioner

4380 Memorial Drive – Suite 100
Decatur, Georgia 30032
(404) 298-4000

WE CARE . . .

Our goal is to provide timely and courteous service.

In order to help us evaluate our service to you, please list the date and time you arrived at the Tag line and see that each person that serves you notes the time you arrived at their station.

Cust Arrival Date: _____   Time: _____

Screener: _____   Time: _____

Cashier: _____   Time: _____

- -

Please assist us in ensuring that your tag/title application is error free. . . Verify all information before signing. Thank you!

LET   US   KNOW   HOW   YOU   FEEL   ABOUT   OUR   SERVICE!

	Very Good	Good	Fair	Poor
Quality of Information Received	☐	☐	☐	☐
Courtesy	☐	☐	☐	☐
Speed of Service	☐	☐	☐	☐
Overall Satisfaction	☐	☐	☐	☐

Additional Comments: _____

_____

_____

_____

_____

Customer Name (Optional) _____

Please drop completed form in Comments Box or mail to address listed above. Thank you!

Motorv/Forms/Service

Being on purpose with integrity

Integrity is doing what you say you are going to do, "walking the talk." If your primary purpose, as stated to your customers, is to provide excellent service on time, but your actual Measure of Success is how much profit you make, you are out of integrity and in reality, it looks like the diagram below which shows a weak service flow.

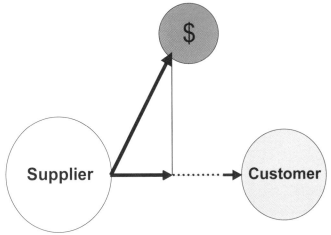

With Pull Thinking however, it looks quite different. Here the primary purpose is customer service. Both service flow **and** financial flow can be maximized.

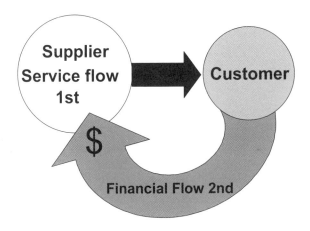

If the measurements your business takes are not defined in your Measures of Success, the possibility for resonance with your customer is limited. The common definition of business automatically lowers the customers' expectation of service. Your customers aren't concerned with your business's profit even though customers know that businesses exist to make money. Reeducating your customers is part of the challenge when the profit motive is replaced with Ultimate Service! Customers will, often through trial and error, gravitate to the business with the best service.

Most businesses are simply not aware of their customer's opinion of them – their perceived value. If the business is profitable today, they might not care. This not caring attitude becomes visible when an Ultimate Service Flow Pull Structure is clearly defined, and all customers and suppliers have discussed and have reached agreement on the answers to the Four Pull Questions.

Key questions include:

- Is the customer the focal point? Does the arrow pointing to the customer actually point to the customer?
- Are the customer's measurements stated in their Measures of Success the same as the supplier's measurements?
- Is this true for both internal and external customer/supplier interfaces? If not, alignment resonance cannot occur. Be absolutely certain on this point.

Individual responsibility and performance reviews

When a true Service Flow Pull Structure is developed, individual employees know their customers and suppliers. Everyone, including managers, can be both a customer and a supplier. At times managers will be customers to those they manage (for example, when fulfilling requests from employees). The term "facilitative management" appropriately describes this role.

Distinguishing employees, departments and teams, as both customers and suppliers will show employees a clear picture of where they fit into the overall Service Flow Pull Structure. Ideally this will serve as the basis for performance reviews. The frequency will vary with respect to the customer and supplier. Manager reviews are often best on a quarterly basis while departmental, team, and employee measures may be as often as hourly, daily, weekly, or monthly. Determining the appropriate frequency is discussed in Step 6.

Because my teammates were working for achievement of specific and attainable goals, which they knew would lead to victory most of the time, they became intent on performing better.... All of us began concentrating on performance in ways that we could see, feel, and measure. And we did it not for money, but for performance! What we wanted was success, and we knew it came in the so-called small plays—the plays that everybody on the team could measure."
—Fran Tarkenton [3]

In the following series of five diagrams, we see a more complex example of a Service Flow Pull Structure for a generic soda company. As we step through each purpose, you can see how individual team members and their performance responsibilities are connected to the overall structure.

The first diagram shows the basic service flow from consumer through the soda manufacturing process to the external suppliers. In this process, the link "to create bottles of Generic Soda" is the weakest link and is highlighted in gray.

---

[3] Tarkenton, Fran, *Playing to Win*, HarperCollins, 1984

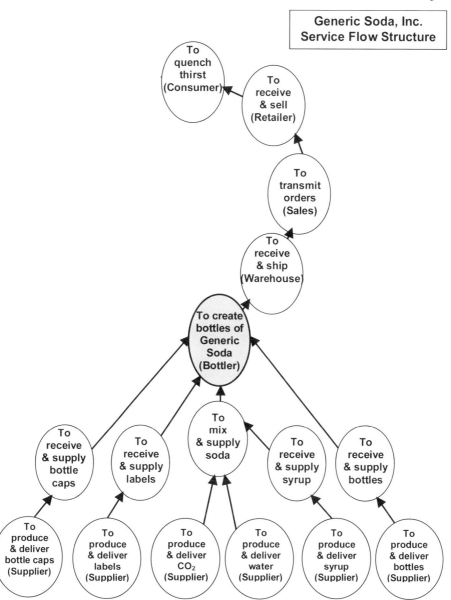

Generic Soda, Inc.
Service Flow Structure

The second diagram shows the link "to create bottles of Generic Soda" exploded to show its team members, which are shown here as more links. Also shown is the supporting Service Flow Pull Structure directly linked to the soda bottling link. The link "to label and supply bottles" is the weakest link in this part of the process and is highlighted in dark gray.

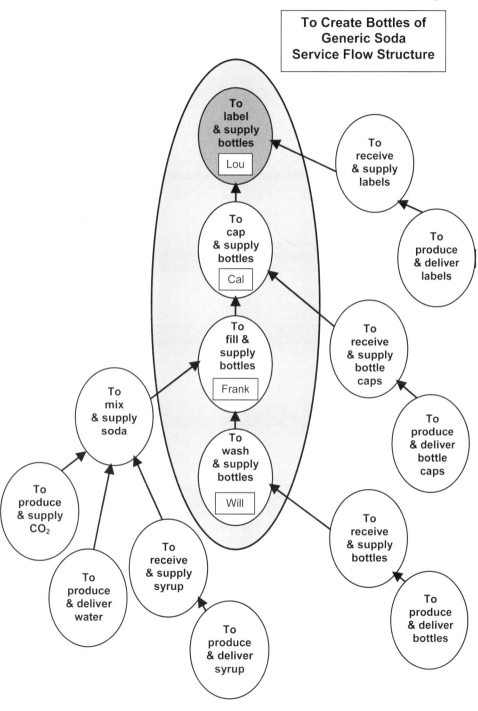

To Create Bottles of
Generic Soda
Service Flow Structure

In the third diagram, the Four Pull Questions are answered for this weak link. As you can see, the Purpose and Measures of Success are very clear with the Purpose shown above the answers to Questions 2, 3, and 4. The measurements and frequency of measurements are written across from each applicable Measures of Success. The first measure listed, 2A, "1st label on a roll is good quality," proved to fall short of the customer's need. What happened was that the customer (the storeowner) received a shipment that contained a skid of bottles with poor quality labels. The printing was smudged on every bottle. What went wrong?

Since only the first label was being checked, remaining defects would go undetected. It was assumed that if the first label was of good quality, then the rest would be good also. That assumption was not true, however, and pointed to a need for a change in measure.

To Label & Supply Bottles
<u>Pull Definition</u>

1. Purpose

To apply only excellent quality labels, uniformly-aligned, and permanently adhered to the correct bottle.

2. Measures of Success:	3. Actual Measurements:	4. Frequency of Measurements:
1st label on roll meets spec	Quality specification met (Yes / No)	At each new roll of labels
Each bottle has the correct label for its contents	Correct label present (Yes / No)	At each new roll of labels & each beverage changeover
Each bottle label is aligned per specification	Alignment specification met (Yes / No)	Each bottle
Each bottle label is overlapped per specification	Overlap specification met (Yes / No)	Each bottle
Each bottle label is adhered to bottle per specification	Adhesion specification "Y" met (Yes / No)	Since test is destructive, bottles must be sampled at X%.
Overall process measure is 6 sigma	No. of defects (ppm)	Each defect

The fourth diagram shows a change in the first Measures of Success. In order to align to the customer's Measures of Success, the Measures of Success was changed to a Cpk measure of greater than 2. As long as the Cpk is greater than 2, then all of the labels on a role are good quality as measured by the supplier or vendor. The Generic Soda Company now needs only to note that the Cpk measure is greater than 2.

Cpk is a Statistical Process Control measure often used to provide 99.999 percent assurance defects are within specification limits. Thus the new and improved, better aligned Measures of Success is shown in the first line.

To Label & Supply Bottles
<u>Pull Definition</u>
Rev. 1

1. Purpose		
To apply only excellent quality labels, uniformly-aligned, and permanently adhered to the correct bottle.		

2. Measures of Success:	3. Actual Measurements:	4. Frequency of Measurements:
Vendor's Cpk print quality value is > 2	Roll print quality (Cpk)	At each new roll of labels
Each bottle has the correct label for its contents	Correct label present (Yes / No)	At each new roll of labels & each beverage changeover
Each bottle label is aligned per specification	Alignment specification met (Yes / No)	Each bottle
Each bottle label is overlapped per specification	Overlap specification met (Yes / No)	Each bottle
Each bottle label is adhered to bottle per specification	Adhesion specification "Y" met (Yes / No)	Since test is destructive, bottles must be sampled at X%.
Overall process measure is 6 sigma	No. of defects (ppm)	Each defect

The 5th diagram shows an additional column at the right indicating, who is responsible for the Measures of Success. This is who needs the measurement and is responsible for taking action to ensure success. As you can see, the Label Applicator Operator is measuring and thus is responsible. This is the team member who takes the label roll and checks to ensure that the supplier certifies a CPK greater than two. If so, then the roll is loaded on the label applicator equipment.

Also note that at the bottom of the Measures of Success list is a Six Sigma Measures of Success. The creation of a bottle is a team responsibility and thus the Team Leader is listed as the responsible person for their team Six Sigma process measurement.

Using this format, individual performance reviews become very easy. Self-measuring now allows the team members to be successful every day vs. once or twice a year in a supervisor's review process.

Since creating a Service Flow Pull Structure and defining Pulls helps identify responsibility for tasks, Pull Thinking is an excellent tool for creating Standard Operating Procedures very quickly.

To Label & Supply Bottles
Responsibility

1. Purpose			
To apply only excellent quality labels, uniformly-aligned, and permanently adhered to the correct bottle.			
2. Measures of Success:	**3. Actual Measurements:**	**4. Frequency of Measurements:**	**Who needs the measurement so they can take responsible action?**
Vendor's Cpk print quality value is ≥ 2	Roll print quality (Cpk)	At each new roll of labels	Label applicator operator
Each bottle has the correct label for its contents	Correct label present (Yes / No)	At each new roll of labels & each beverage changeover	Label applicator operator
Each bottle label is aligned per specification	Alignment specification met (Yes / No)	Each bottle	Label applicator operator
Each bottle label is overlapped per specification	Overlap specification met (Yes / No)	Each bottle	Label applicator operator
Each bottle label is adhered to bottle per specification	Adhesion specification "Y" met (Yes / No)	Since test is destructive, bottles must be sampled at X%.	Label applicator operator
Overall process measure is 6 sigma	No. of defects (ppm)	Each defect	Team leader & team members

Another way to establish Measures of Success is to look at what is being measured. External customer comment cards and internal reports are two resources. These comment cards are usually located in a holder near the exit door. From the Blockbuster comment card shown on the following page, the following Measures of Success could be deduced:

- Success is that every customer is very satisfied with their overall experience when they visit Blockbuster Video.
- Success is that every customer is very satisfied with the service received from the customer service representatives.
- Success is that every customer is very satisfied with the time it took to check out.
- Success is that every customer is very satisfied with the appeal of the store environment.
- Success is that every customer is very satisfied with the availability of the products they look for.
- Success is that all customers who have other comments about Blockbuster write them on the comment cards.
- Success is that all customers who want a response regarding their comments write their name and phone number on the comment cards.

We can assume that the desired frequency is "every customer," since there is no indication of frequency of measure. However, it's likely that only a small percentage of customers actually send the cards back. Of those, 95 percent are complaints. So how can Blockbuster get a better measure? They might consider giving the customer an incentive to provide feedback (other than a negative experience!) For example, they might print the card information on the receipt slips, along with a free rental coupon offer for either returning the comment card or calling an 800 number to speak to a Blockbuster customer representative. Another option would be to have service representatives in the store hand each customer a comment card with the free video rental offer one day each month.

HOW ARE WE DOING?

Each of us here at **BLOCKBUSTER** is empowered, authorized and expected to take care of you. Please take a few moments and let us know how you were treated today.

| | **Very Dissatisfied** | | | **Very Satisfied** | |
	1	2	3	4	5
Overall, how would you rate your experience at BLOCKBUSTER during your last visit?	❏	❏	❏	❏	❏
How satisfied were you with the service you received from the customer service representative?	❏	❏	❏	❏	❏
How satisfied were you with the time it took to checkout?	❏	❏	❏	❏	❏
How appealing was the store environment to you?	❏	❏	❏	❏	❏
How satisfied were you with the availability of the product you were looking for?	❏	❏	❏	❏	❏

Comments: Date of Store Visit: _____

_____

_____

_____

_____

If you would like a response to your comments, please fill out the following:

Name: _____ Phone: (_____) _____

Drop this postage paid card in the mail and your feedback
will go directly to the Regional Director of Operations for your area.

BLOCKBUSTER name, design and related marks are trademarks of Blockbuster Inc. ©2000 Blockbuster Inc. All Rights Reserved.

13099

In the following example, Measures of Success are written together with the vision and mission of a quality team in an electronic assembly company.

The head of the Quality Assurance (QA) department did a great job of defining the Vision, Mission, and Measures of Success for his department team.

Test and Quality Assurance Vision Statements:

A.   We are a provider of excellent products and services because:

B.   We are applying "Total Quality Management" principles that deliver "Zero Defect" products and services to our customers.

C.   We are providing our internal customers with products and service that they can rely on.

D.   It is our belief that "Excellence" is a way of life and we demonstrate "Excellence" everyday through:
1. Effective Leadership
2. Individual Integrity
3. Commitment to Continuous Improvement.

E.   Established partnerships with key vendors help to yield higher productivity because we are better educating them on our quality requirements.

F.   We are the leaders and trendsetters that make this company the single best choice for our customer.

Test and Quality Assurance Mission Statements:

G.   To provide every customer, internal and external, with a product that meets or exceeds the published specifications, is reliable, is available to ship on or before the required date, is the best value available and promotes customer enthusiasm every day.

H.　　To establish a manufacturing environment that provides for continuously improving the quality and efficiency of our services and establishes trust and respect for each individual by enlisting only team members that choose to share and participate in our Vision and our Mission.

I.　　To better educate vendors about our expectations of quality and service through written correspondence (fax, mailed letters etc.), site visits, electronic mail and telephone.

J.　　To continuously measure and improve each other's performance as well as the teams performance, our vendor's performance and customer satisfaction.

Daily Measures of Success:

1.　　Customers experience our service as being courteous, helpful and respectful 100 percent of the time.

2.　　Employees begin their workday by or before 7:00 a.m. and end their workday by or after 4:30 p.m. every day.

3.　　Employees observe proper lunch breaks, 11:30 a.m. to 12:30 p.m., every day.

4.　　Employees maintain a clean and organized work area throughout each workday.

5.　　We complete 100 percent of incoming materials inspections by 8:30AM and document problems/rejects on the daily operations flip chart or the RTV (Return to Vendor) form when the product warrants returning to the vendor.

6.　　We achieve our production goals by 4:30 p.m. or earlier, individually and collectively as a team.

7.　　Customers receive products and service on or before their agreed upon requested date 100 percent of the time.

Weekly Measures of Success:

1. We accurately document, review and deliver our time sheets to Accounting by 9:00 a.m. each Monday.
2. We evaluate and improve our efficiency by comparing the number of hours worked against the standard hours scheduled and chart both individual and team performance.
    - 100 percent efficiency is excellent.
    - 90 percent efficiency is good.
    - 80 percent efficiency is fair.
    - 70 percent or lower efficiency is poor.
3. Vendors receive written specifications, drawings and performance criteria as orders are placed and realize the following:
    - "Zero" defective part/ part number is excellent.
    - "One" defective part/part number is fair.
    - "Two" or more defective parts/part numbers is poor.
4. We compile the number of rejects and problems, by purchase order number, part number, quantity and defect and report this information back to our vendors along with their rating.

Monthly Measures of Success:

Customer Service Expectations are:
1. Product returns are evaluated, documented, repaired and returned within 72 hours.
2. The quantity and defect of returned products are charted and all trends are analyzed, root cause determined and corrective action taken within 3 working days.
3. Customer perceives our integrity as impeccable 100 percent of the time.

On the surface, this looks like a complete Vision/Mission and Measures of Success statement with daily, weekly and monthly frequencies of measurements. It appears that all Four Pull Questions have been answered. But putting this (as best as we can) into a Service Flow Pull Structure reveals a clearer picture. In the following flow structure diagram; we see each Vision and Mission statement inside the links. The Mission statement J for example contains one Mission, but it applies to four categories: individual, team, vendor, and customer. Each Mission was then given a separate link: J1, J2, J3, and J4.

Mission Statement "J"

To continuously measure and improve each other's performance as well as the team's performance, our vendor's performance and customer satisfaction.

Next, each Measure of Success was applied to the appropriate Vision or Mission. Some measures were applied to multiple Vision or Mission statements if appropriate. Monthly measures were coded M, weekly W, and daily D. If there was no measure found for a Vision or Mission statement, the link was not shaded and the link was given a dotted line to signify an incomplete Pull. The shaded links have measures and are defined Pulls, thus having a much higher possibility of successful service.

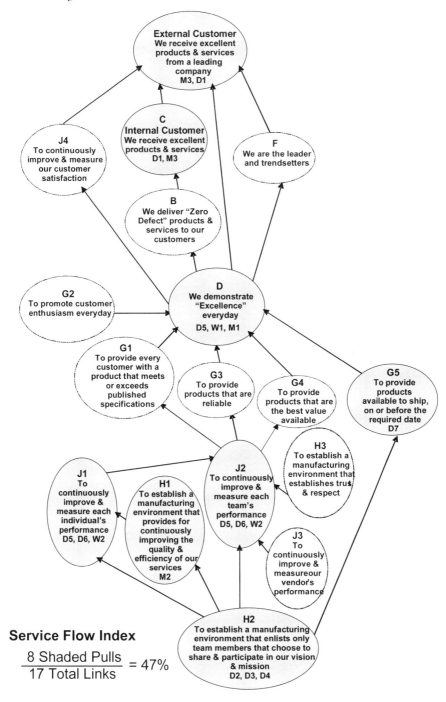

Service Flow Index

$$\frac{8 \text{ Shaded Pulls}}{17 \text{ Total Links}} = 47\%$$

For shaded links that are separated by an un-shaded link, the lower shaded link has a high probability of being frustrated. Since the link being served had no Measures of Success defined, these purpose links are in the Trial and Error process. There are 9 un-shaded links and 8 shaded links out of a total of 17 links. One could say that this Service Flow Pull Structure has a 47 percent possibility (8 shaded links divided by 17 total links x 100) of being successful in achieving Ultimate Service resonance. This is a very useful measure on service flow possibility called the Service Flow Index. This highlights the importance of constructing a Service Flow Pull Structure in order to get a handle on the size of the gap between where your business is now and your Vision of achieving Ultimate Service resonance.

In weekly measure number 1, the Accounting team was addressed. There was no Vision or Mission specifically addressing Accounting because Accounting is one of the several internal customers addressed in Vision C and Mission G. Internal supplier/customer teams like Accounting, Maintenance, Janitorial Services, or Administrative Services, and all internal suppliers or service providers are often also internal customers who need information in order to perform their service.

This same customer/supplier relationship occurs between two people having a conversation. When you are listening to another speaking you are a customer receiving the communication. The roles are reversed when you begin to reply and become a supplier of communication.

The diagram below shows one way to show the internal supplier/customer relationships in a Service Flow Pull Structure. It also shows investors and stockholders as suppliers to the organization, supplying support in the way of money to be acknowledged with returns on their investment.

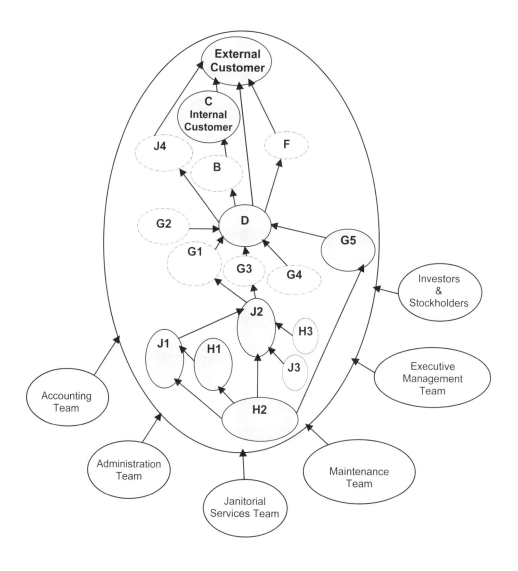

Example using a menu of measures of success

Below is a menu of ideas for team leader Measures of Success. This provides ideas for a team leader, CEO, VP or any manager to discuss with their team (their internal customers) and ask them to reach a consensus on which 8 to 10 measures are the most important. Measures of Success stated in this manner could use a measurement scale of 1 – 10 with 1 being "Strongly Disagree" and 10 being "Strongly Agree."

---

1. Primary Purpose: To provide team leadership and support

2. Success is that:

I provide support without removing responsibility

People feel and act empowered

Everyone on the team looks forward to working together

100% of team works together in harmony

There is very open communications among all team members

There is professional respect between all team members

Team morale is rated a 10

Service Flow Index is 90% or greater

I ensure that the individual team member Service Flow Index is 90% or greater

Team members have specific purposes and clear measures of success

Team member contributions and ideas are recognized and rewarded

I ensure that accomplishment of team and individual goals are met 100% each month

I am on time 98% of time

I give both positive and negative feedback when appropriate

I hardly ever create undue priorities

I foster an environment of trust and respect for one another

I create a positive work environment

I ensure mutual accountability all the time

I do what I said I will do

I respond very quickly to questions and concerns

I am trustworthy

I set priorities with agreements and respect others priorities

I maintain a rich understanding of all projects in my purview

I ensure continuous improvement

I am excellent at developing people

Menu of Ideas for Measures of Success
(Choose 8 – 10 that are the most important)

Example: Looking at Measures of Success to solve problems (to reduce turbulence)

The following example may look easy, but when different methods or tools are used to measure the same thing, trouble is in the wind.

I was the newly hired Production Manager at an electronic equipment manufacturer. There was a huge problem with rejects on one product, a TV infrared remote control.

Our supplier would test every infrared device they shipped us, but when we installed it into the product at our plant, there was a failure rate of over 30 percent. This meant a big rework cost to us. This problem had existed for over a year before my time, costing us well over $200,000.

We could not prove that the infrared devices were defective, so our process included a certain percentage of rejects. The boards, with the defective infrared device soldered into them, were stockpiled and waiting to be repaired at a later date. The defective device problem caused a large pile of boards to accumulate. Once the cost was quantified on monthly accounting reports, there was a great deal of pressure on us to resolve the problem.

Using Pull Thinking, I simply began asking if we were both using the same testing device. The answer was no.

The Quality Assurance manager and I paid a visit to the supplier bringing our test device. Sure enough, the results showed that both devices measured the same. We were puzzled and went back to our company still looking for the answer.

It wasn't until two weeks later that I happened to overhear a conversation with the electrical design engineer. The distance between the receiver and the circuit board infrared sending device was to be six feet according to the specification that the engineer had written. However, the engineer mentioned something about using a lens to change the testing distance. The problem, it turned out, was that the supplier did not have a lens in front of the infrared device but there was a lens in front of the device when it was installed on the circuit board at our plant. This meant that what we thought were defective devices probably weren't. The test should have been performed at a distance of four feet, since a lens was being used. The specification simply didn't cover both conditions!

In the end, we learned that the supplier was giving us good parts and we were rejecting them because we had applied the standard erroneously. A new standard was written and the reject pile was retested and put back into production. All of them passed! We saved hundreds of thousands of dollars by not scrapping the parts.

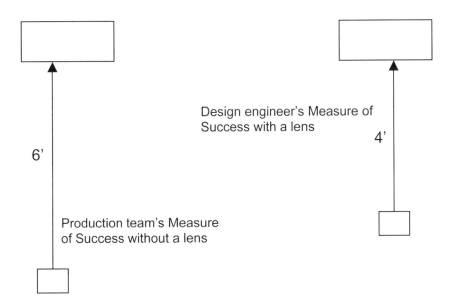

Design engineer's Measure of Success with a lens

Production team's Measure of Success without a lens

I discovered the answer by listening for agreement on the Four Pull Questions. When I heard the engineer talk about lenses and distance differences I knew a solution was near. There was not agreement on the second Pull question – the Measure of Success. There was agreement on Pull questions 1, 3, and 4.

Another example involves a cookware manufacturer. After years of producing an electric frying pan and many happy customers, the reject level was running at twenty-five percent. The profit margin wasn't high enough to cover the rework costs. After many efforts to improve the problem with little success, the company considered discontinuing the line. This would mean less work, layoffs for the employees, and lost revenue for the company. The customer would also lose when the product was no longer available.

As the senior industrial engineer at the time, I asked that we have a meeting to discuss other possible solutions before the final decision was made. At the meeting, I asked, "Who knows the specification measurements on the line at present? Where is the specification book located?" The answers were that 1) the supervisor didn't know the specifications very well; and 2) the specification book was in the office collecting dust. There was no accountability and no written documentation on the measurement results.

Then I asked, "Who knew the specifications on the line during the first year it was being produced?" The answer was that the supervisor knew and worked closely with the manufacturing engineers at that time. This meant that the measurements (Pull Question 3) in the specifications were being performed up to the point when the supervisor was changed. The Measures of Success were very clearly written in the specification.

It became obvious that at present no one was applying the specification measurements. They were simply fixing problems; trial and error methods were in full bloom. The problem was addressed; the original supervisor was assigned who knew the specs; the reject level was greatly reduced; and the line was not shut down! This saved thirty jobs in the plant, preserved the revenue flow, and the product was still available to the customer.

The reality of the day-to-day rush of activities had muddied the picture and this simple answer was hidden from view. Getting back to basics was not addressed as a solution because it was being assumed that the basics were covered.

I looked for who was responsible for applying the specifications listed in the book. The measures were there; they just weren't being applied. The frequency was zero. A quality product was created as a result of a supervisor being responsible. The supervisor got promoted and other supervisors were assigned to the product line. Managing people became the issue and the product specification responsibility became eroded. Decay set in and death of the product was in process.

Asking the Four Pull Questions changed that outcome for the better for everyone involved.

Step 5
The Third Pull Question
Determine the Actual Measurements

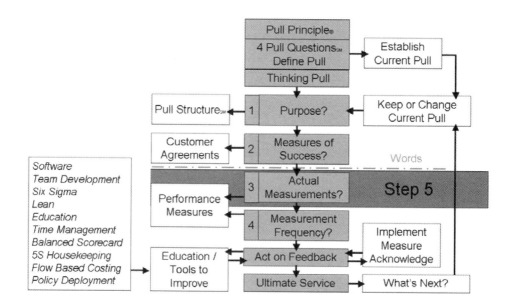

Pull Thinking Process

What are the actual measurements being taken?

We constantly measure—both consciously and subconsciously. We measure our speed to make sure we aren't driving too fast or too slow. We measure the time to make sure we aren't late for a meeting or waiting too long for our meal at a restaurant. We measure our change to make sure we didn't overpay. Each of these measurements provides needed feedback to help us accomplish our purpose and keep our process in control. Our actions are framed by feedback from the measurements with our purpose in mind.

Taking actual (physical) measurements assures awareness of what is Pulling, and keeps us pointed in the right direction.

At the same time, our customers are constantly measuring our service to them. They notice if we did what we said we'd do, if we returned their phone call promptly, if their order was filled correctly, if their shipment was on time, if their name was spelled correctly on an invoice, and so on. Customers' experience of service is the sum of these types of measurements.

To truly be in alignment with our customers, we need written, visible shared measurements. Writing them down for everyone to see assures that customers and others have shared expectations, integrity is ensured, and everyone has the opportunity to support your process of continuous service improvement. This is how Pull Thinking begins to build resonance and inspire passion in people.

What to do first becomes clear—talking to customers and getting their feedback. This does two things:

- It lets your customer know how well you are serving them.
- It lets you know how your service rates with your customer.

With Pull Questions 3 and 4, the reality of the vision or mission sets in for both the customer and the supplier. The line in the sand has been drawn with the answers to Questions 1 and 2. Now it's time for your business, your team, and yourself to take a stand, to let everyone know you mean business. Otherwise, there is nothing to support, no game to play—only talk.

The clarity that comes from taking a stand takes the noise away allowing everyone to focus, to start playing the game of service. When we answer Questions 3 and 4, we take a stand.

By defining and sharing the measurements, you are saying that you are willing to take the action necessary to make improvements because you care about both your internal customers (teammates and co-workers) and external customers. The act of taking the measurements focuses your attention. The more frequent the measurement, the sharper the picture becomes, and the more attentive everyone becomes. Taking measurements and displaying the results is for the world to see and choose to support or not support. A stand is visible. Put it in writing.

Source of measurements

Measurements come directly from Measures of Success, and ensure accomplishment of Purpose.

Change the Measures of Success if a measurement is not aligned to the purpose or if the frequency of measurement is actually zero (meaning the measurement is not made). Rarely would one start with the answers to the first two Pull Questions and not have to revise the answers to Questions 3 and 4. Since we're not accustomed to thinking in this manner, we have a habit of saying our intentions and then going about doing what we intended without actually taking measurements very often. Here's an example of applying a measurement in a project environment:

Q1 What is the Purpose? The purpose is to provide a weekly progress report		
Q2 What are the Measures of Success?	Q3 What are the actual measurements?	Q4 How often will the measurements be made?
Success is that the weekly progress report is turned in by the end of the week.	A scale ranging from beginning to end of when the weekly report was produced	"Weekly progress report" is referred to in Question 2. This is the answer to Question 4 or at least a place to start to determine the appropriate "how often" to measure

Question 1 – purpose, Pulls Question 2 – the intended Measures of Success, which Pulls Question 3 – actual measurements, which Pulls the action of—Question 4 – how often the measurements are made (the frequency of measurements). This could be improved by a more frequent, daily check on the report progress by the compiler in order to prevent being late. Frequency will be covered in greater detail in Step 6, but some discussion is necessary in this step due to the difficulty in talking about measurement without referring to its frequency.

The question is often asked: What is the difference between Pull Questions 2 and 3?

When you move from Pull Question 2 to Pull Question 3, you cross the line from the "thought world" to the "physical world"—the difference between *talking* about something and *actually doing it.*

Pull Questions 1 and 2 are "talking about it"—defining it and visualizing it.

Pull Questions 3 and 4 are all about "actually doing it."

By definition, a measurement is used to quantify something in order to establish a point of reference that in turn provides the basis for making choices about actions in support of making improvements towards creating something. The measurement itself, however, does not have much meaning. For example, knowing that you're going 45 miles per hour in a car only has significance when you know what the speed limit is. Automobile speed limit laws put Measures of Success (context) to the actual measurements of automobile speed on public roads.

Measures can be shared and easily communicated.

When you establish an Ultimate Service Flow Pull Structure as discussed in Step 3, you'll likely learn that you have more internal and external customers than you previously thought. This is fine for your own personal business, but it needs to be communicated when others are involved—such as co-workers, team members, customers, suppliers, for example. It is important and necessary to write it down. Real communication in Pull Thinking is written so others can see it, relate to it, and support it.

It's likely you are constantly taking measures subconsciously.

Taking measurements frequently with more customers (internal and external) will cost more time and energy in the beginning. There will be time spent talking to customers getting agreement on measures and asking questions about their service experiences. There are often many more types of customers to discover and to talk to. Long term, however, this is far less costly than the costs of solving problems created when the Four Pull Questions are not answered.

"An ounce of prevention is worth a pound of cure."
—Benjamin Franklin, *Poor Richard's Almanac*

The high cost of losing a customer

Measuring the Cost of Losing a Customer

- For every customer who bothers to complain, there are 26 others who don't.
- 91 percent of unhappy customers will not return.
- The average "wronged" customer will tell 8 to 18 people.
- If you make an effort to remedy customers' complaints, between 82 percent and 95 percent will come back to you.
- It costs about five times as much to attract a new customer as it costs to keep an old one.

From studies conducted by Washington, D.C. Technical Assistance Research Programs, Inc.

Although this study focused on external customers, the same data can also be applied to internal customer service issues. The important point to remember is that even if you don't measure customer service, your customers will.

When getting agreements with customers, keep in mind the four basic types of measurements. By definition, the most precise measurements are objective and direct.

Four types of measurements

Objective measurement is: having to do with a known or perceived object or service to be measured as distinguished from something existing only in the mind. It is independent of the mind; real; actual, determined by and emphasizing the features and characteristics of the object or service being measured, perceptible to others. Using values such as: numbers of people, length in feet, number of dollars, time in minutes, number of times late to a meeting, number of completed projects, etc.

Subjective measurement is: produced by the mind resulting from the feelings or experience of a person's thinking; not just rigidly reflecting reality. Using scales such as: excellent – poor, very satisfied – not satisfied, on time – never on time, scale of 1 – 10, etc.

Direct measurement is: honest and to the point; straightforward; frank, with nothing or no one between; immediate; close, or firsthand. Talking to customers face to face or providing a form for customers to provide written feedback on their service experience, is an example of a direct measurement.

Indirect measurement is: secondary or lagging behind in time or a reflection of something being caused by what you are measuring. Like driving your car by only looking in a rear view mirror to see where you have been. Financial measurements used to measure service experience of customers, using the feedback from a small percentage of customers to estimate the service experience of all customers, observing customers without talking to them and assuming by their actions the service experience they are having, are all examples of indirect measurements.

For example:

← ——— Better

Direct objective	Direct subjective	Indirect objective	Indirect subjective
Production assembler's own daily rating on # of defects per 100 opportunities	Production assembler's own daily range of poor to excellent quality	Inspector's weekly rating on # of defects per 100 opportunities	Quality rated by customers' monthly feedback on a range of poor to excellent quality
Percentage of on-time delivery of products or services weekly	Service provider's feelings about being on time: almost never to always, measured weekly	Sample study on customers to determine % of on time delivery for the past year.	Customers' feelings about being on time: almost never to always, measured yearly
Self measured monthly performance review with numerical values like # of commitments completed, etc.	Self measured monthly performance review with scale of satisfactory to unsatisfactory	Manager measured annual performance review with numerical values like # of commitments completed, etc.	Manager measured annual performance review with scale of satisfactory to unsatisfactory

Characteristics of good measurements

- It's important and agreed to by the customer – enroll the customer
- As objective and direct as possible
- Results can be validated – reproduced consistently by others
- Can be improved upon – if you can't possibly improve the result, change the measurement to one that can be improved upon
- Simple and understandable
- Practical and economical to measure
- Quick and easy to do—don't make it a burden for the customer to provide the measurement data, or the feedback form difficult, long, or inconvenient
- It gives timely feedback, allowing identification of a problem before the process goes out of control; a leading measurement

Creating a Pull environment requires patience and tenaciousness with the process. It's important to find the best answers to Pull Questions 2 and 3. The best measurements will give you the best, most useful information. Over time, new technology and new ideas provide better measurement possibilities and will of course result in a change in the Measures of Success.

Ultimate measurements

When creating Ultimate Service, it follows that an ultimate measurement must be sought. Start with:

Don't do it the other way around! That limits the creativity to finding ways of getting a "thank you" or making money instead of creativity in finding different ways of being service-minded, which is a wellspring of infinite possibilities. Service creativity flows from being service minded. The highest possible service to a customer is the result of ultimate measurements. Ultimate measurements are best defined by your customer. But customers may have difficulty saying it, since ultimate service is not a common event today. But customers know ultimate service when they experience it. What do you do? Talk to your customer and brainstorm about just what ultimate means to them.

Another way is to look at examples of ultimate measurement systems such as Six Sigma, Malcolm Baldridge National Quality Award, and (International Standards Organization) ISO 9000. These are excellent for getting ideas about what "ultimate" measurements are.

Six Sigma simply means a measure of quality that strives for near perfection. Six Sigma is a disciplined, data driven approach and methodology for eliminating defects (driving towards six standard deviations between the mean and the nearest specification limit) in any process in any type of business including manufacturing products and providing services.

Malcolm Baldridge Award winning companies are known for:

- Visionary leadership
- A focus on customer and market knowledge and customer relationships
- High performance work systems and employee education and development
- Clearly designed and well-managed processes for products and service delivery
- Strong financial and market results

ISO 9000 – When a large majority of products or services in a particular business or industry sector conforms to International Standards, a state of industry-wide standardization can be said to exist. This is achieved through consensus agreements between national delegations representing all the economic stakeholders concerned - suppliers, users and, often, governments. They agree on specifications and criteria to be applied consistently in the classification of materials, the manufacture of products and the provision of services. In this way, International Standards provide a reference framework, or a common technological language, between suppliers and their customers - which facilitates trade and the transfer of technology.

There are many resources on measurement, two of these are:

1. The Research Methods Knowledge Base, by William Trochim, Ph.D., Cornell University, available as an online edition or paperback. This is a comprehensive text for undergraduate and graduate social science research courses.

2. A Dictionary of Units of Measurement, written by Russ Rowlett, Director, Center for Mathematics and Science Education, University of North Carolina at Chapel Hill. This is an online dictionary on metric units of measure available only at: www.unc.edu/~rowlett/units/index.html

The chart on the next page highlights the Measures of Success from the Ultimate Service Flow example from the wood shop in Step 4.

- 100 pieces of wood,
- 12" long,
- 6" wide Oak,
- painted dark blue,
- loosely packed in a box,
- delivered every 2 days.

These are their team's ultimate direct objective measures.

The actual measurements (Q3) for these measures have been added. (The frequency (Q4) is certainly part of the ultimate measurement and will be added in Step 6.)

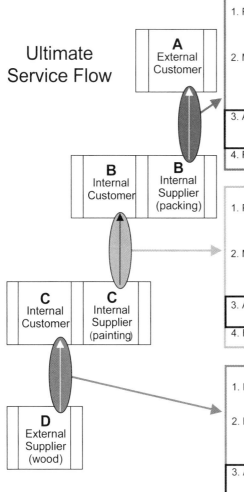

Ultimate Service Flow

A — External Customer

B — Internal Customer

B — Internal Supplier (packing)

C — Internal Customer

C — Internal Supplier (painting)

D — External Supplier (wood)

Pull on B by A
1. Purpose:
   To pack & deliver cut and painted wood.
2. Measures of Success:
   Success is 100- 12" long, 6" wide pieces of oak, painted dark blue, and loosely packed in a box, are delivered every 2 days.
3. Actual Measurement:
   Tightness of pack on scale of 1 to 5; 5=very tight, 1 = very loose
4. Frequency of Measurement:

Pull on C by B
1. Purpose:
   To paint cut wood.
2. Measures of Success:
   Success is 100- 12" long, 6" wide pieces of oak, painted dark blue, are delivered every 2 days.
3. Actual Measurement:
   Color (from color chart)
4. Frequency of Measurement:

Pull on D by C
1. Purpose:
   To supply cut wood.
2. Measures of Success:
   Success is 100 pcs. of oak cut 12" long 6" wide, are delivered every 2 days
3. Actual Measurement:
   a. # of pieces of wood, # feet in length, # feet in width
   b. # days between wood deliveries
4. Frequency of Measurement:

The chart below summarizes this service flow example.

	Question 2	Question 3			Question 4	
Action	Success is:	What to Measure	Type of Measure	Frequency	Who is the Customer	Who is Measuring? Responsible?
Provide	100 pcs. of Oak,	#pcs. of wood	Direct, Objective		Internal Customer C	External Supplier D
Cut	12" long,	# of Feet of Length	Direct, Objective		Internal Customer C	External Supplier D
Cut	6" wide,	# Inches of Width	Direct, Objective		Internal Customer C	External Supplier D
Paint	painted dark blue,	Color	Direct, Subjective		Internal Customer B	Internal Supplier C
Pack	loosely packed in a box,	Tightness of Pack	Direct, Subjective		External Customer A	External Supplier B
Deliver	delivered every 2 days,	If Delivered	Direct, Objective		External Customer A	External Supplier B
Receive	received every 2 days.	If Received	Direct, Objective		The Public Customers of Ext. Cust. A	External Customer A

Who's responsible?

The answer to this question lies in another question: "Who's taking the measurement?" These are two very important questions. The answer to both questions is the same. It is the one who's Pull it is, the one who is asking the Four Pull Questions. That's who takes the measurements. That's who's responsible for providing and improving the service flow.

Whether an individual, a team, or group, the Pull of the flow of service is owned by the one actually doing the measurements. One can request that the measurements be taken by others. But in the eyes of Pull, the requester is still the one taking the measurements and the one being responsible.

Measurement system examples

It follows then that the responsible person or team must have the authority to provide the service as well as authority to take action to improve the service when needed. This is a self-measured process, not a managed or *"someone else"* measured process. The drawing below shows the difference between a managed trial and error process and a self-measured preventive process. The shortest, least mistakes made, smoothest ride process is obvious. Clear responsibilities are defined by who is taking the measure. Self-measure produces self-responsibility and builds passion for performance.

Managed	Self-measured (Pulled)
Wait for others to say what to do	I am motivated to learn
Not responsible	I own it
Seldom see the effects of my contribution	I can see the effects of my contribution
Acknowledged mostly if there are mistakes	Acknowledged with or without mistakes

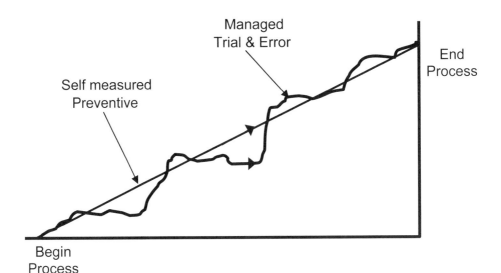

Direct measurements on service experiences are leading measurements, compared to profit and sales data. Profit and sales measurements are lagging (indirect) measurements on customer service, since they "follow" products and services being provided. Therefore, directly measuring service experience will give you better real-time actionable feedback than measuring financial data so that you can actually affect the financial outcomes.

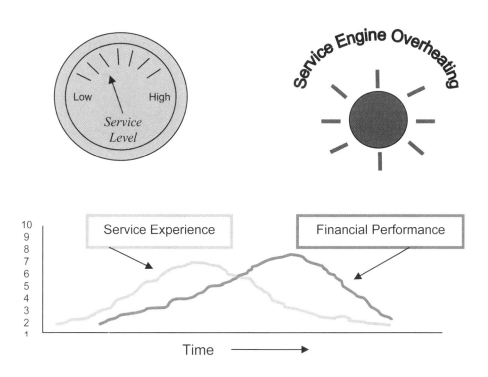

Accountants are no more responsible for the financial service flows (profit, loss, pricing, and so on) than a quality control inspector is for product rejects—or no more responsible than is a reporter for an auto accident on which he's reporting. An accountant is responsible for the accurate measurement and reporting of financial flows.

Those requesting the financial measurements and reports: various government organizations, managers, executives, and teams, for example, are the responsible decision makers. Accountants can also be responsible for showing how financial flows affect other financial flows and helping us understand what financial problems need attention.

There may be times when the internal measurement system is out of alignment with the customer. For example: The president of Company Z has to make a choice between spending $420,000 this year for either new computer hardware or additional human resources in the IT department. The executive bonus system is based on the level of profit margin achieved each year.

Spend $420K on hardware	Spend $420K on IT headcount
7 year amortization	Immediate cost impact
Reduces profit $60K / year	Reduces profit $420K this year
Minimal effect on customer service	Increases customer service
Easier to make profit target and earn executive bonus	Harder to make profit target and earn executive bonus

In this example, there is great pressure on the president to spend the money on hardware instead of human resources. As a result, there is pressure to let customer service suffer at the expense of making the profit number. The Measure of Success regarding profit measurements is at odds with the Measure of Success for the improvement in services the business could realize.

Changing the president's bonus plan from a profit measurement to an improved customer service measurement would remove the pressure and align his actions with the customer. Actions that improve customer service will trigger many areas that cause profit improvements. But this is hard to quantify and thus often not as favored as actions that have a more directly calculable effect on profit.

Combine this with the traditional accounting systems that do not depict true costs and you face a hidden problem and missed possibilities.

Many businesses utilize a Balanced Scorecard system to ensure that focus extends beyond financial matters. It helps to align business strategies with measures, reducing this kind of stress on executives and management teams. Usually applied at a high level in organizations, the Balanced Scorecard still emphasizes achieving financial objectives while monitoring measures on customers, internal business processes, and learning and growth.

In Pull Thinking, the emphasis is on achieving an appropriate balance between all measures at all levels.

The Service Flow Pull Structure created using Pull Thinking automatically produces a natural "balanced scorecard." The balance in business must be between two measures: customer service and acknowledgement of service (financial measures) with respect to each individual, team, department, and to the business itself. The kind of balance that results in Pull Thinking is a natural result. The Balanced Scorecard is a good step in that direction.

The question is: What is the definition of balance?

Is it simply that each of the four areas is being addressed? Is it that there are an equal number of measurements? Or, is it that the percentage of compensation (acknowledgement) tied to each category is equal?

Some organizations create the appearance of using a Balanced Scorecard by talking about each area. In reality, they may unwittingly throw the scorecard off balance when more compensation is placed on financial measures than the other three combined (customers, internal, learning, and growth).

In contrast, Pull Thinking has the customer on top, followed by internal process, then learning and growth, with financial at the bottom serving as the root system infusing the life blood of financial revenue and profits throughout the whole organization.

Remember, customers' primary concern is not about your profits. But they do *want* to be able to count and depend upon you. They want to be loyal to a brand that provides Ultimate Service. They know that if they're going to depend on you for excellence, you have to be there. They'll provide the lifeblood, money. Why? Because you've emphasized balance. They support you because you provide excellence.

How can you be sure? The answer again is simple. Ask. Measure.

Enroll your customers

Here are some examples of "enrolling statements" found on comment cards and survey forms:

Satisfaction survey: "Thank you for sharing your experience and ideas with us."

Your opinion at work: "At Physician Group Z, we are concerned about the quality of care and services that you receive from physicians participating with us. Your opinions are very important. In fact, they become part of a quality measurement system used to evaluate your physician. Please take a few minutes to answer the attached questions. Although you may have filled out a questionnaire like this in the past, please do so again. Your answers will be treated as strictly confidential."

Feedback: "Thank you for taking the time to give us your feedback so we may have a healthier environment. If you prefer, you may call us at 1-800-xxx-xxxx."

"Please help us serve you better: Your opinion matters to us! We would appreciate your feedback regarding today's visit to this restaurant. Please fill out the attached questionnaire and return it for a FREE Breakfast menu item."

"How are we doing?"

"Did we deliver?"

"This is not a comment card. It's a direct pipeline to the top. We're happy you stopped by our business, and we want to make sure you'll come back. So, if you've got a little time, we'd really appreciate it if you'd fill out this card and drop it in the mail. Your comments and/or suggestions are extremely important to us and will go directly to our President. And if you can't tell him what you think, whom can you tell?"

"HELP! Your total satisfaction means everything. Your comments make a difference."

You've seen the statement above on similar external customer comment cards and questionnaires in most businesses. What you don't see are internal customer comment cards and questionnaires. This is where the work is often needed when establishing an Ultimate Service Flow resonance.

You can't hide actions; they speak too loudly. So why would one need to hide the measurement results? Display the measurements for all to support. *Service with integrity* is displayed and ensured.

Measurements and marketing surveys

Sometimes, businesses use a service measure form that includes marketing survey questions like: How many children do you have? What is your income level? What products do you plan to buy in the next year?

This does not belong on a service measurement form.

Sure, we understand and appreciate that marketing data is important, but it should be a separate form because it serves a very different function and will confuse the real purpose that you want your customers to communicate—the service experience. This undermines your message of caring for the customer and, worse, it looks like a smoke screen. If you must, put these questions at the end and address them as optional so customers can choose to ignore them after completing the service experience questions.

I plan to publish a book of a collection of measurement forms that I have accumulated over the past 12 years. In the meantime, there are other great resources: *The Balanced Scorecard* by Robert S. Kaplan and David P. Norton, and *The Six Sigma Revolution* by George Eckes. Other Six Sigma books provide good examples of subjective measures for many different types of services. The book *Best Practices in Customer Service* by Ron Zemke and John A. Woods is another excellent resource. Also, ISO 9000 and the Malcolm Baldridge Award illuminate measures on attributes of excellence in business.

What if there is no measurement, no unit of measure? Benchmark what others are measuring. Look around for similar service measurements. Ask your customers.

Two points to remember:

It's more than just asking questions, ones needs to "get dirty" with your customers and work along side them. If you can, observe what they do with your product or service. That way, you can uncover measurements that may better support their needs.

Customers can say what they need, but ultimate service broadens into more specific measurement detail regarding their needs.

You don't always need to ask, just observe. Reading non-verbal measures people display is a skill that is always useful to know, but the accuracy of interpretation is dependent upon your experience and whether or not the customer is genuine in displaying non-verbal signals.

The type of scale can influence the accuracy of measurements. Use a scale of 1 to 5 instead of 1 to 10. According to the late Dr. Rensis Likert, an eminent professor of management from the University of Michigan, studies have shown that because there is a lower probability of people using the whole range of numbers on a 1 to 10 scale, people usually use the extremely high or extremely low numbers. There is a higher probability of all the numbers being used on a 1 to 5 scale. Also, placing the highest or best end of the range first balances out the tendency of being accustomed to complaining vs. acknowledging great service.

Important points about customer service measurement systems:

- Group customers with similar measures.
- Thank your customers when they communicate.
- Reward customers when appropriate, for example, give a free meal for being the 100th customer to fill out a service experience form. Or give a gift, a chance to win a prize.
- Be precise.
- A measurement system should support the process of improvement, analyze, define solutions, improve, and control.
- A few key performance measurements in the hands of many throughout the organization is much more empowering than hundreds of performance measurements in the hands of a few in top management.

Examples of measurement application:

Test and Quality Assurance Team example

Let's continue the Test and Quality Assurance Team Measures of Success example from Step 4. Here are measurements that could be derived from the Measures of Success statements, including the frequencies, who is responsible and suggested type of form:

Test & Q. A.
Daily Measures of Success:

1. Customers experience our service as being courteous, helpful and respectful 100 percent of the time.

Measurement: percentage of time – being courteous, helpful and respectful

[These are behaviors that would not be written but noted mentally by the Q. A. team everyday but I suggest also adding this to their monthly internal customer measure form.]

2. Employees begin their workday by or before 7:00 a.m. and end their workday by or after 4:30 p.m. every day.

    Measurement: yes or no – work begins and ends on time twice a day – once at beginning and once at end of day.

    [This could be written on a chart by the Q. A. team member everyday but suggest also adding this to their quarterly performance reviews. Most likely, the daily measurement would not be done unless someone was late or quit early. The team members would comment or communicate dissatisfaction in a non-verbal manner. If a time clock is used, the measure would be certain.]

3. Employees observe proper lunch breaks, 11:30a.m. to 12:30p.m.

    Measurement: yes or no – work begins and ends on time twice a day – once at beginning and once at end of lunch.

    [Noted mentally by team members. Most likely, this daily measurement would not happen unless someone was often late or quit early, the team members would comment or communicate dissatisfaction in a non-verbal manner.]

4. Employees maintain a clean and organized work area throughout each workday.

    Measurement: on two scales: 1 to 5 with 5 being most organized and 1 to 5 with 5 being very clean.

    [This would be better as a weekly or monthly measurement posted on a wall chart by the team leader. Also, a 5-S system of measurement would be a more rigorous measurement.]

5. We complete 100 percent of incoming materials inspection by 8:30 a.m. and document problems/rejects on the Daily Operations flip Chart or the RTV (Return to Vendor) form when the product warrants returning to the vendor.
    Measurement: percentage inspected by 8:30.
    Measurement: yes or no – problems/rejects noted.
    [Team members could write both of these measurements on the flip chart.]

6. We achieve our production goals by 4:30 p.m. or earlier, individually and collectively as a team.
    Measurement: percentage of production goal met.
    Measured once per hour on a flip chart by team members.

7. Customers receive products and services on or before their requested date 100 percent of the time.
    Measurement: percentage of time all customers receive products on time – written on a flip chart by team members. [Frequency may also vary depending on the type of service. (i.e., a request that takes 3 days to complete would need an hourly or daily measure to ensure completion within 3 days.) *This would be better as a weekly or monthly measurement.*]

Weekly Measures of Success:

1. We accurately document, review *and* deliver our time sheets to Accounting by 9a.m. each Monday.
   a. Measurement: percent accuracy of documentation of time on time sheets.
      [The best would be for each employee would record their own time 1/day at end of day and review 1/week. This would be a mental check and not posted.]
   b. Measurement: yes or no, if reviewed 1/week by supervisor.
      [This would be a mental check and not posted.]
   c. Measurement: time delivered to Accounting.
      [This could be posted for all to see.]

2. We evaluate and improve our efficiency by comparing the number of hours worked against the standard hours scheduled and chart both individual and team performance.
   - 100 percent efficiency is excellent
   - 90 percent efficiency is good
   - 80 percent efficiency is fair
   - 70 percent or lower efficiency is poor.
     a. Measurement: percent efficiency of individuals
        [By individual team members and post on flip chart.]
     b. Measurement: percent efficiency of team
        [By individual team members and post on flip chart.]
     c. Write evaluations of *excellent to poor* on flip chart 1/day, by team leader and members.

3. Vendors receive written specifications, drawings and performance criteria as orders are placed and realize the following:
   - Zero defective parts/ part number is excellent.
   - One defective parts/part number is fair.
   - Two or more defective parts/part numbers is poor.

    a. Measurement: number of defective parts/part number – on each   defective vendor part by QA team member. Frequency is each event when a defect occurs. Write in a logbook or on a wall chart.

    b. Measurement: Yes or No, did vendor receive specifications drawings and performance criteria with each order. To be done by a Purchasing team member who places the order. Frequency is each event when order is placed. Write in a logbook or on a wall chart.

4. We compile the number of rejects and problems, by Purchase Order Number, Part Number, Quantity and Defect and report this information back to our vendors along with their rating.

    a. Measure: Yes or No, were rejects and problems compiled for each purchase order number – by QA team member as a check off item on a reminder check list on the wall.

    b. Measure: Yes or No, were the rejects compiled by part number, quantity and defect.

    c. Measure: Yes or No, was the information reported to the vendor along with their rating – by QA team member as a check off item on a reminder check list on the wall and in a vendor logbook.

Monthly Measures of Success:

Customer Service Expectations are:

1. Product returns are evaluated, documented, repaired and returned within 72 hours.

    a. Measurement: Yes or No, a customer returned product was evaluated – on a checklist sheet attached to returned product by QA team member. Frequency is per event of product return.

    b. Measurement: Yes or No, a returned product was documented – on a checklist sheet attached to returned product by QA team member. Frequency is per event of product return.

    c. Measurement: percent repair is complete – on a wall chart and an evaluation sheet attached to returned product by QA team member. Frequency is per event and 1/day.

    d. Measurement: number of hours since returned product was received and date product was returned to the customer – by QA team member. The frequency would be per event and 1/day written on a wall chart.

2. The quantity and defect of returned products are charted and all trends are analyzed, root cause determined and corrective action taken within 3 working days.

    a. Measurement: Yes or No, quantity and type of defect is charted mental note by QA team member per product return event.

    b. Measurement: Yes or No, defect trends were analyzed and written on wall chart – by QA team member per product return event.

    c. Measurement: Yes or No, root cause of problem was determined and written on wall chart – by QA team member per product return event.

    d. Measurement: # of days, since return was received and written on wall chart – by QA team member and team leader per product return event and 1/day. Also write corrective action taken and date.

3. Customer perceives our integrity as impeccable 100 percent of the time.

    Measurement: percent of time customers perceives impeccable integrity in our service – written on a wall chart by QA team leader as a summary from customer survey forms included with each customer delivery.

Executive level example

It's equally important to measure the non-financial service aspects of executive level positions. Although at present we're not accustomed to defining it, as we evolve into the future, service measures will become commonplace.

In this example, the customers of the vice president of franchise development were first identified in the Service Flow Pull Structure below and coded in order to easily associate them to each of their appropriate measures of success statements.

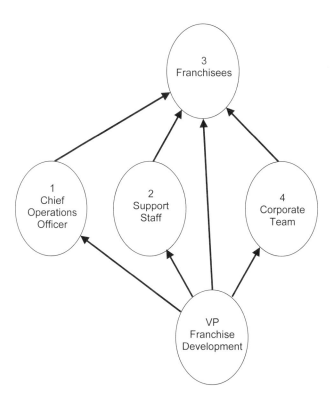

Next, a form was used to show how all Four Pull Questions were used to identify the role of the VP in the organization.

Customer Code		Q2 Measure's Of Success	Q3 Measurement	Q4 Frequency
Q1 Purpose: To build and lead a qualified and dedicated team of development professionals				
3, 4	1	Franchise openings occur according to monthly plan 100% or greater	% of Franchise openings that occur according to plan	Monthly
4	2	Company monthly openings occur according to plan 100% or greater	% of Company openings that occur according to plan	Monthly
4	3	Capital projects are within + or - 10% of monthly budget	% of monthly budget	Monthly
4	4	Overhead costs are within monthly budget	yes/no	Monthly
3, 4	5	Deliver a facility that will enable a profitable economic business model with a sales:investment ratio of 1.1:1 or better after 1st year	Sales:Investment ratio	Once at end of first year
1, 4	6	Maintain a rich understanding of all projects 100% of the time	% of time having an understanding of all projects	Monthly
	7	Ensure a competent engaged and fully functioning team providing:		
1, 3, 4	7a	Excellent quality franchisee advice monthly	Scale of Poor to Excellent	Monthly
1, 3, 4	7b	100% of projects are on track for planned openings weekly	% of planned openings projects on track	Monthly
1, 3, 4	7c	Provide excellent weekly communications	Scale of Poor to Excellent	Monthly
1, 2, 3	8	Provide excellent leadership, coaching and development to the Development Services Team	Scale of Poor to Excellent	Monthly
1, 2, 4	9	Assure that accomplishment of team and individual goals are met 100% each month	% of goals met	Monthly
1, 2, 3, 4	10	Ensure that professional standards of architecture, construction and real estate are met or exceeded 100% of the time on each project	% of time professional standards are met	Each project

This was a starting point for refining the measurements and developing measurement forms. After discussion with the customers, "Excellence" was defined for the measurements in 7a, 7c, and 8.

7a	7c	8
Attributes of Excellent franchisee advice:	**Attributes of Excellent weekly communications:**	**Attributes of Excellent leadership, coaching and development:**
Provides information leading franchisees to make good decisions that prevent problems.	Communications are clear, complete, concise, honest and open, to the point, and on time. Excellent communications are always given to the appropriate parties that either should receive it or need it.	Excellent development is providing thorough knowledge and experience that results in one feeling fully capable of using and empowered with the skills needed and learned.
Facilitates planning for change.		Excellent leadership is providing forward vision and focus
		Excellent coaching helps one see what they can't see and guides them to be self-directed and self-empowered, to align talent with vision.

From this point, measurement forms were made and again discussed with the customers to establish agreement and to alert them of how often they will receive the forms to be filled out. Once that was done, the first measurement was taken. The Pull started!

There are several combinations of customer measurement forms to be made. Since all measurements do not apply to each customer, and each measurement is not on the same frequency, it is necessary to combine other measurements from other members and teams into as few forms as possible for each shared customer. This example shows that a monthly measurement form is needed for customer code #4, the corporate team. The form developed for the corporate team customer (ultimately in alignment with the Pull of the stockholders of the company) does not include measure #5 because it is at an annual frequency and #8 because it does not apply to the corporate team.

VP Franchise Development monthly self-measurement form	Month _____
1 What % did franchisee monthly openings occur according to plan?	% _____
2 What % did company monthly openings occur according to plan?	% _____
3 What % did capital projects come within + or - 10% of monthly budget?	% _____
4 Were overhead costs within monthly budget?	yes/no _____
6 What % of time did you experience rich understanding of all projects from our team	% _____
7a What was the quality of franchisee advice this month? (summarized from measurement form given directly to franchisees that received advice)	
Excellent ___Above Ave. ___Average ___ Below Ave. ___Poor ___	
7b What % of the projects were on track for planned openings?	% _____
7c What was the quality of franchisee communications this month? (summarized from measurement form given directly to franchisees.)	
Excellent ___Above Ave. ___Average ___ Below Ave. ___Poor ___	
9 What % were individual and team goals met this month?	% _____
10 What % of time were professional standards of architecture, construction and real estate met on each project?	% _____

Auto service example

Below is a good example of a customer "request for feedback" letter. This was received one week after car service:

Thank you for allowing our trained technicians at ... ... to handle the recent service needs of your Jaguar. We appreciate your confidence in giving us an opportunity to work on your vehicle.

Within the next month, you will be receiving a survey from Jaguar as part of a Service Follow-up about your experience at .... Please take a moment to answer these questions, as this is our Report Card and represents how professionally we handle your needs. Please understand that this survey <u>does not</u> represent your vehicle or Jaguar Cars of North America. It is strictly <u>our</u> Report Card and grades us with Jaguar as to our performance.

Our #1 Goal is for you to be **Completely Satisfied**, have an **Excellent Service Experience**, to **Strongly Agree** on your overall opinion, and you **Definitely Would** recommend .... as a place to purchase, or have a vehicle serviced. If there is anything we can do to serve you better, let us know. We are always looking for new ways to excel.

This letter is part of our Service Follow-up, so please call me if you have any questions or problems at all concerning your service visit. We look forward to being able to serve you again.

Thank you,

Measures of quality, efficiency and productivity

Hour	Minutes	Start	Actual # of Oper.	Actual # of ManHrs	Unit Shipped Goal	Unit -# Goal	Unit Shipped	Unit -# Shipped	Minutes Down	Team Pass	Problem/Comment
									Std # on team =	9	
									Std Units/shift =	5	
1	60	7:00	8	8.0	1	-17	0		30		Rework rivets
2	60	8:00	8	8.0			1	-17			
3	60	9:00	8	8.0	1	-17					
4	60	10:00	8	8.0			1	-9		1	
5	60	11:00	8	8.0	1	-17	0			-1	
6	60	12:30	8	8.0	1	-9	1	-9			
7	60	1:30	8	8.0			0				
8	60	2:30	8	8.0	1	-9	1	-9		-1	
OT		3:30		0.0							
TOTAL	480			64	5.0		4.00		30	-1	
		Takt Time/Hr =		1.3						25%	(% Rejects)
		Linearity =		0.80							
		% Productivity =		89%						1%	(% Downtime)

Down Time Codes:

% Down			% Down	
TM = Team Meeting			UMR = Unknown Source Material Reject	
OS = Out of Stock			TR = Training	
VMR = Vendor Material Reject			EP = Equipment Problem	
PMR = PDU Material Reject			FTR = Final Test Reject	
			O = Other	

This report is from a manufacturing production team. They recorded their own information on a flip chart each day. This report was used to capture the flip chart information in digital format to save the information and to provide visible measurements to anyone not on the production floor. The report contains these hourly measurements:

- Number of team members (operators) working
- Goal number of units to ship
- Number of units shipped
- Number of minutes of down time
- Number of team passes (number of units passed on to the next team member in line with a mistake)

For daily team performance measurements, the report measured these issues:

- Percent Productivity
- Takt time (average number of hours between shipped units)

- Linearity (the percentage of match to the production goal for the day)
- Percentage of time spent during the day on these issues:
  - Team meetings
  - Out of stock
  - Vendor material reject problem
  - Team self-generated reject problem
  - Unknown source material reject problem
  - Training time (time lost due to training)
  - Final test reject problem
  - Other problems listed
  - Total time spent not producing
  - Total time spent on reject problems

Next, is an example of a Skill Level Bullet—a visible self-measurement on a production team member's skill learning progress toward their goal. There are seven different skills this operator needs to learn in order to be a fully cross-trained team member. There are four levels: Beginning in black; Advanced in dark grey (able to produce excellent quality with assistance); Certified in grey (able to produce excellent quality without assistance); and Trainer in light grey (able to train other team members). Team members proudly display their progress towards accomplishing their vision.

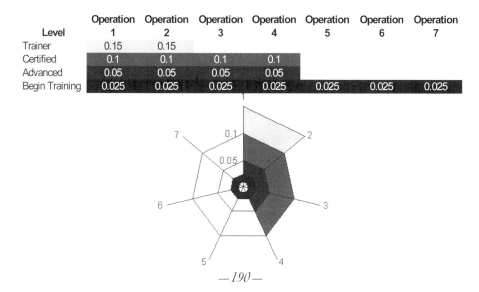

Level	Operation 1	Operation 2	Operation 3	Operation 4	Operation 5	Operation 6	Operation 7
Trainer	0.15	0.15					
Certified	0.1	0.1	0.1	0.1			
Advanced	0.05	0.05	0.05	0.05			
Begin Training	0.025	0.025	0.025	0.025	0.025	0.025	0.025

Below is a photo of a communication board showing photos of the team members with their Skill Level Bullet measurement.

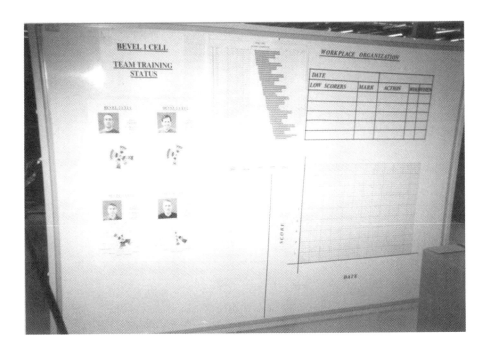

Difficult objective measurements require some creativity

When it is difficult to put the measurement into words, a drawing or photograph can serve as a comparison standard or benchmark type of measurement. In the example below two small scratches in a painted wood panel are acceptable. Any damage over that is defined as a reject and must be repaired or scrapped, i.e. three or more small scratches or two scratches longer than the two on the left are all rejects.

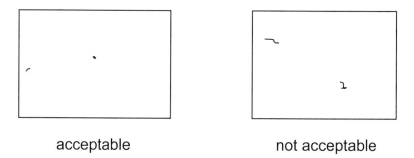

acceptable   not acceptable

Example of a company president

Below is a collection of measures for evaluating the President of a business from the book *Flight of the Buffalo*[1]:

Great Performance for the President

1. Coach of strategic thinking
   Measure: Number of helpful contributions I make to the strategic thinking of others. Indicated by member / customer evaluation of the president in the monthly surveys. A rating of 10 on a scale of 1 – 10 is expected.

2. Learning and growth
   Measure: Attainment of 100 percent of the president's educational goals.

3. 100 Percent of the people believe they own the right problems and are capable of handling it.
   Measure: As indicated by ownership comments on the weekly reports.

4. Coach of personal development. Facilitator of learning for everyone in the company.
   Measure: 100 percent of direct reports attain 100 percent of their educational goals and report complete satisfaction with their development. 100 percent of all employee-partners attain 100 percent of their educational goals and report complete satisfaction with their development.

5. Ensure that all transactions are characterized by caring and integrity.
   Measure: Measured by employee responses of being important, respected, valued, and cared about personally on the quarterly all-employee survey. Other indicators are number of personal messages exchanged, number of personal celebrations acknowledged.

---

[1] Belasco, James A. & Stayer, Ralph C., *Flight of the Buffalo*, Warner Books, 1993

Customer service measurement examples

The next several pages contain examples showing various communications measuring success. By putting the phrase "success is..." in front of each item listed and assuming that the best aspect of the range is success (like excellent, yes, or totally satisfied), you will have the actual Measures of Success statement. What is not known here is the frequency of measurement.

DEAR VALUABLE CUSTOMER,

We would like to hear your comments about this Center and how you feel we can make it a better place for you. By focusing on Customer Satisfaction, we strive every day to exceed your expectations. Please take this opportunity to fill in and return the attached card with your comments and suggestions. Your comments will assist us in providing you with even better service in the future.
Thank you for helping us to serve you better.

Customer Service Department

	Excellent	Good	Average	Poor
Please rate your shopping experience at our Center.	❑	❑	❑	❑
Please rate the level of customer service in our Center.	❑	❑	❑	❑
Please rate the level of cleanliness in our Center.	❑	❑	❑	❑
Please rate the level of value found in our Center.	❑	❑	❑	❑

What stores or services would you like to see in our center? ....

What was your most enjoyable experience at our center today? ....

Do you have any general comments or suggestions that would make this center a better

place for you to shop? ....

How did you first hear about our center? ....

Your Total Satisfaction
Means Everything.
Your Comments Make A Difference

The Store	Excellent	Above Average	Average	Below Average	Poor
Overall shopping experience	○	○	○	○	○

The Merchandise

	Excellent	Above Average	Average	Below Average	Poor
Selection	○	○	○	○	○
In stock	○	○	○	○	○
Value	○	○	○	○	○

The Sales Personnel

	Excellent	Above Average	Average	Below Average	Poor
Sales people available	○	○	○	○	○
Sales people knowledgeable	○	○	○	○	○

The Checkout Area

	Excellent	Above Average	Average	Below Average	Poor
Speed	○	○	○	○	○
Friendliness	○	○	○	○	○

The Service Desk

	Excellent	Above Average	Average	Below Average	Poor
Courtesy	○	○	○	○	○
Helpfulness	○	○	○	○	○

Customer Type   Do-It-Yourselfer ○   Contractor / Commercial Customer ○

Additional Comments:

Optional, but appreciated:
Name
Address

Phone

BEN & JERRY'S

How was your Ben & Jerry's experience? We want to know how we're doing.

1. Was your scooper friendly & cheerful? ☐ Yes ☐ No ☐ Not sure

2. Were we fully focused on getting it just right? ☐ Yes ☐ No ☐ Not sure

3. Did your scooper know all about Ben & Jerry's? ☐ Yes ☐ No ☐ Not sure

4. Was our scoop shop clean & inviting? ☐ Yes ☐ No ☐ Not sure

5. Were you fully satisfied with your purchase? ☐ Yes ☐ No ☐ Not sure

6. Was your visit unique, fun & entertaining? ☐ Yes ☐ No ☐ Not sure

Please use the back to let us know what else is on your mind.

QuikTrip
RESTROOM SURVEY

QuikTrip is conducting a survey of our customers to find what improvements you would like to see in our restroom facilities.

How do you rate QuikTrip's restrooms?

Date _____ Time _____

	Excellent	Satisfactory	Unsatisfactory
Cleanliness	☐	☐	☐
Adequately Stocked	☐	☐	☐
Security/Privacy	☐	☐	☐
Fixtures (toilets, sinks, etc.)	☐	☐	☐
Quick Accessibility	☐	☐	☐
Overall Impression	☐	☐	☐

If you could make any changes to the restrooms what would it be?
(More lights, more stalls, private restrooms, different fixtures, etc.)

Loan Process Evaluation

Please indicate your level of satisfaction with each of the following aspects of your Bank of America loan using the scale below:

		Totally Satisfied	Satisfied	Somewhat Satisfied	Neither Satisfied nor Dissatisfied	Somewhat Dissatisfied	Dissatisfied	Totally Dissatisfied
1	The simplicity of the application process.	☐	☐	☐	☐	☐	☐	☐
2	The speed of the application/approval process.	☐	☐	☐	☐	☐	☐	☐
3	All necessary documentation was requested within a reasonable time.	☐	☐	☐	☐	☐	☐	☐
4	The clarity of explanations and answers to your questions regarding the loan.	☐	☐	☐	☐	☐	☐	☐
5	Being kept informed throughout the loan process.	☐	☐	☐	☐	☐	☐	☐
6	The time it took from application until the loan closing.	☐	☐	☐	☐	☐	☐	☐
7	The closing documents were ready at the time committed.	☐	☐	☐	☐	☐	☐	☐
8	The clarity of the closing instructions in the closing documents.	☐	☐	☐	☐	☐	☐	☐
9	The process of obtaining your loan, overall.	☐	☐	☐	☐	☐	☐	☐
10	The value of your home (as estimated by us) compared to what you felt it was worth.	☐	☐	☐	☐	☐	☐	☐

11 Please estimate the number of days it took from the time of application until the time of the loan closing.

☐ YES   ☐ NO

12 Were the terms in the closing documents what you had expected?

13 How likely are you to use us again the next time you need a loan?   ☐ 100% ☐ 80% ☐ 60% ☐ 40% ☐ 20% ☐ 0%

Use the reverse side for any additional comments

PLEASE RETURN IN THE POSTAGE-PAID REPLY ENVELOPE PROVIDED.

WELCOME TO
LOGAN INTERNATIONAL AIRPORT

Please help us to serve you better by taking a moment to fill out this card. Your comments and suggestions are reviewed carefully to improve our services. Please put this card in the suggestion boxes located throughout the terminals. Thank you for your help.

Thomas J. Kinton, Jr., Director of Aviation

AIRPORT IN GENERAL

	Excellent	Good	Fair	Poor
Employees: available, courteous, helpful	( )	( )	( )	( )
Overall cleanliness	( )	( )	( )	( )
Rest room facilities: clean, well-marked	( )	( )	( )	( )
Terminals: attractive, clean, comfortable	( )	( )	( )	( )
Parking facilities: convenient, clean	( )	( )	( )	( )

MASSPORT INFORMATION BOOTHS (lower level):

Well-marked, courteous, helpful service	( )	( )	( )	( )

SIGNAGE well-marked, concise, clear directions

Roadway	( )	( )	( )	( )
Parking	( )	( )	( )	( )
Terminals	( )	( )	( )	( )
Ground Transportation	( )	( )	( )	( )

GROUND TRANSPORTATION convenient, clean, efficient:

Airport Shuttle buses	( )	( )	( )	( )
Logan Express buses	( )	( )	( )	( )
Taxis/Limousines	( )	( )	( )	( )
Airport Water Shuttle service	( )	( )	( )	( )

This form includes an "Importance to You" column on the left in order to help the business set priorities for improvements. This is an excellent idea especially for a new business.

Customer Service Report Card

ΠΙCRO CENTER
THE COMPUTER DEPARTMENT STORE

"Our most valued customers are the ones who give us their opinions."

Importance to You:				Micro Center's Grade:				
Very Important	Important	Of Less Importance		Strongly Agree	Agree	No Opinion	Disagree	Strongly Disagree
❏ ❏ ❏			The store was clean	❏ ❏ ❏ ❏ ❏
❏ ❏ ❏			The products were easy to find	❏ ❏ ❏ ❏ ❏
❏ ❏ ❏			Sales people were readily available	❏ ❏ ❏ ❏ ❏
❏ ❏ ❏			Sales people were polite and friendly	❏ ❏ ❏ ❏ ❏
❏ ❏ ❏			Sales people were knowledgeable	❏ ❏ ❏ ❏ ❏
❏ ❏ ❏			Sales people suggested the items I needed	❏ ❏ ❏ ❏ ❏
❏ ❏ ❏			Checkout was reasonably quick	❏ ❏ ❏ ❏ ❏
❏ ❏ ❏			My sales receipt was complete and accurate	❏ ❏ ❏ ❏ ❏
❏ ❏ ❏			I felt my purchase was a good value	❏ ❏ ❏ ❏ ❏
❏ ❏ ❏			I felt welcome in Micro Center	❏ ❏ ❏ ❏ ❏
❏ ❏ ❏			I would recommend Micro Center to others	❏ ❏ ❏ ❏ ❏

Okay, we've covered the third of the Four Pull Questions and the many aspects of measurements. We know about the purpose of Measures of Success and measurements in a Pull environment, what ultimate measurements are and where you find them, their characteristics, and the ownership of responsibility. The frequency of measurements is the last but perhaps the most important aspect of the Four Pull Questions. For what good would all those measures be without the appropriate Frequency?

Step 6
The Fourth Pull Question
Determine the Frequency of Each Measurement

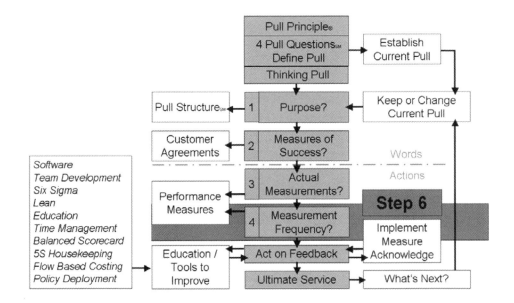

Pull Thinking Process

New hopes, new styles, and most important, a new way of
seeing. Revolutions do not come piecemeal. One account of
nature replaces another. Old problems are seen in a new light
and other problems are recognized for the first time
— James Gleick.[1]

What is the frequency with which the measurements are being taken?

This is the last of the Four Pull Questions. Frequency affects almost everything. For example, how often, on the average, do you want words to be printed on this page?

Once

        every

                  six

                                inches?

Or   twice   an   inch?

Or once an inch?

Once an inch is the obvious natural resonant frequency in this example.

---

[1] Gleick, James, *Chaos: making a new science* Penguin Books, 1987

Another example of resonant frequency is how often you have staff or team meetings. Are they held once a week or once month? What if the frequency of need is not regular (linear), but is non-regular or chaotic (non-linear)? Do you still have weekly meetings?

We often force regularity onto non-regular needs because it's the best system we know. Looking then at service and financial flows, should service and financial flows be measured with the same frequency—say every month or every three months? Or should they be measured when needed, just in time?

The example on the facing page shows two similar businesses with the same current revenue and profit. Both appear to be delivering a similar level of customer service. Both have hired a new customer service employee.

As the frequency of measurement is increased, it becomes clearer which business is benefiting from great service from the recently hired employee.

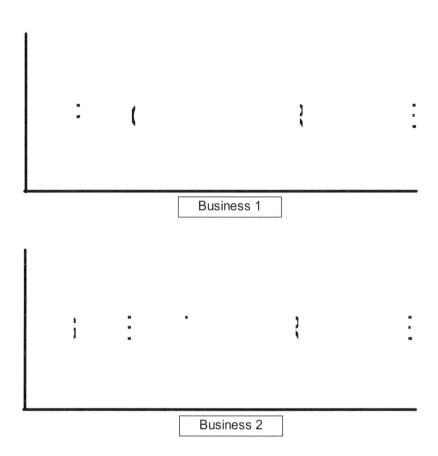

Measuring once a week doesn't show us anything about the quality of service.

POOR SERVICE

Business 1

GREAT SERVICE

Business 2

Measuring once a day shows more and *almost* reveals the differences in their service levels.

POOR SERVICE

Business 1

GREAT SERVICE

Business 2

Measuring every four hours in this type of business shows that Business 2 had great service. This is the resonant frequency of measurement for Ultimate Service, since it allows you to make distinctions between poor and great service.

The frequency (rate of measurement) is something that must be consciously and carefully chosen and then practiced with discipline and regularity. Choosing the frequency creates the last important definition on the desired behavior to support the purpose. Taking the frequency to 0 means no measurement is being done and no feedback is gained, so no proactive improvement is possible. The Pull force goes to 0.

Frequency brings power and passion elements to Pull. The strength of the Pull in business is fed by shared passion supported by frequency. Take the frequency to "0" and the Pull and shared passion will stop!

Passion from purpose Pulls passion for frequency. They feed each other. Establishing the appropriate measurement process in the beginning supports and sustains a sometimes-fading passion of purpose as time goes by. Since the initial passion lives day to day in the measurement process, it is very important to establish a good measurement process. Passion can be seen in the speed of improvement resulting from the focus on improvement that frequency of measurement can bring. What is the resonant frequency of your shared passion?

Frequency is also a good measure of integrity—since frequency is a measurement on the behavior of the measurement itself. Lower than resonant frequency can be perceived as "lip service," and higher than resonant frequency can be perceived as "obsession" or, if done by your boss, as "micro-management."

Integrity is an important ingredient of passion. Saying that you measure (value) something when measurements actually occur only once in a while or chaotically is not integrity. Not understanding Pull can lead to questionable integrity of the measurement system.

Take, for example, the performance review systems of two businesses. Business 1 conducts them annually, and Business 2 conducts them quarterly. Both claim to value their employees and take actions to make that promise real. But which one puts more energy into expressing that value, as shown by a greater frequency of measuring those actions? What if something is wrong and employees don't feel valued? The company makes positive changes, right? But what happens if the employees are dissatisfied *for an entire year* before management even realizes there is a problem? In the best-case scenario, more than a year passes before circumstances improve. Now then—how long does management wait before they manage the success of the change? Another year?

Integrity of the business or management team can be in question when one knowingly uses an ineffective measurement frequency due to cost cutting efforts aimed at bettering the bottom line.

Frequency empowers you to find solutions

Knowledge is power. The more frequently you measure, the more power you experience. The power lies in the difference between measuring a potential problem area once a year versus measuring once a quarter. In the former scenario, a problem can persist, and grow, for an entire year before it's even discovered. In the latter, at most it can exist for a quarter. It would be better still if your team measured monthly, or even weekly.

This power is magnified in a team environment. The power a team can experience can be compared to the laser light phenomenon. A ten-watt light bulb can produce the same light intensity of a 100-watt light bulb if all of the photons are aligned into one direction, as a laser system does. The more often you measure your service flow, the more alignment possibilities there are in a team environment. Why is the alignment increased? Because the passion of common purpose is being realized and communicated with the frequency of measurement. Frequency of shared measurements Pulls shared passion and shared passion Pulls alignment. In this context people have a *Passion for Performance*.

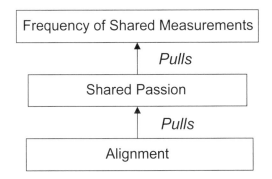

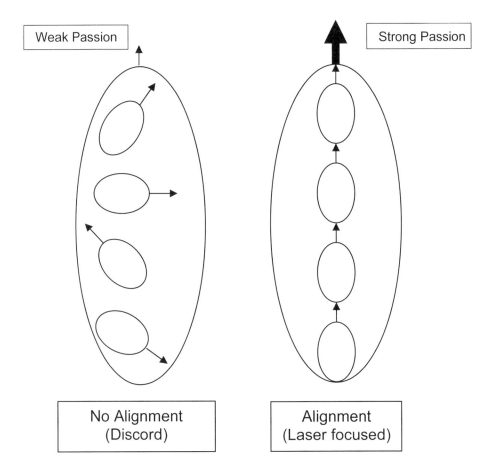

The frequency of measurement keeps us present with our purpose

The frequency of measurement also keeps us aware, thus enabling success in the process. Knowing we are succeeding and accomplishing our purpose is more rewarding—and reduces stress. Employee turnover decreases in an environment of success and acknowledgement. This alone provides a financial business case for creating a Pull Thinking environment.

Cost Estimate of Replacing One High-Potential Manager

Separation Costs	$500
Recruiting Costs	$7,500
Selection Costs	$7,500
Training Costs	$5,000
Lower productivity – acculturation	$10,000
Lower productivity – long term	$25,000
Total	$55,500

Data from *The HR Scorecard*, page 99

The frequency needs to support the Measures of Success. From Step 4:

Attributes of a powerful Measure of Success statement:

- The actual measurement is stated or can be easily determined
- Objective rather than subjective
- Can be applied in terms of a unit of measure such as: percentage, scale (1 to 5 or poor to excellent, for example), feet, pounds, dollars, or miles per hour
- Easy to measure
- Customers and suppliers agree on the value of the measurement
- More specific than general
- Applies to something you can do something about, and take action based on it
- Supports the Vision or Mission statement; brings clarity to the vision/mission
- The frequency of measurement is stated or can be easily determined
- The frequency of measurement is agreed upon by both customer and supplier

---

Purpose is realized through the influence of frequency. French physicist Louis de Broglie said that "as a result of a great law of nature, every bit of energy of proper mass is intrinsically related to a periodic phenomenon of frequency." Albert Einstein said that matter is a form of energy in his Theory of Relativity Equation: $E=mc^2$. Therefore, everything has a frequency associated with it. Three of the building blocks of our universe: nuclear, gravitational, and electromagnetic forces are attractive (Pull) forces with frequencies. "Uni-" in the word "universe" implies one. These forces are unifying forces pulling on all of us. Is there any question that frequency is of utmost importance?

One of the easiest things to change in Pull Thinking is the frequency aspect of the Fourth Pull Question. How often we think or say something makes a difference. Each link in a Service Flow Pull Structure has a frequency. Finding the appropriate frequency is key to seeing results. Too fast or too slow will have dramatically different results. Think of what happens to water when its frequency is changed. When water is heated, the vibration – frequency of movement of molecules of liquid water – is greatly increased until the water becomes steam. If you slow the frequency of the molecular motion down by reducing the temperature below 32 degrees Fahrenheit, the liquid water becomes solid ice.

In business, the flow of service needs to flow like a liquid, not a gas or solid. It needs to flow in a continuous, purposeful direction, like a navigable river or water that produces hydroelectric energy. It must not sit statically, or evaporate away randomly. The frequency of measurement must produce such a flow.

The most frequent measurements in the business world are connected to financial flows. Remember, financial flow is a lagging measurement on service flow. Money flows in and money flows out. Some money doesn't move at all. As discussed in previous steps, the common definition of business is "a primary focus on profit." In that mindset, the frequency of measurement on financial flow is higher than that on service flow.

What if we increase the frequency of service flow measurements to be higher than that of money? Wouldn't service flow become the primary Pull — more powerful than the Pull of money?

What is the appropriate frequency of measurements for service flows? Obviously enough, the answer depends on the kind and type of service. Nonetheless, it should be higher than any lagging measurement frequency, like financial or the size of your customer base. You'll find another answer in your natural passion — and in the passions you want to stimulate in others. Having an overall vision for a business may not translate into passion for everyone. That high-level vision passion is usually achieved with stock options, bonuses, and pay increases tied to financial performance instead of performance towards the overall vision of Ultimate Service. There's a problem here.

Setting the frequency of measurement

The frequency possibilities lie in the different combinations of time, distance, or event gaps between measurements. With history, some trial and error may be necessary to determine the Ultimate Service resonant frequency—measuring every day versus every three days, for example. Do you measure every second or minute or every week or year? It all depends on the service process. When you drive a car down the road, you have to measure many things almost every second to ensure safety.

Each process has a natural or resonant frequency where the measurement supports the purpose for the least cost in time or money.

Resonant feedback frequency

Another use of frequency is to make a flow visible. When you watch a movie, the film images move at a rate of twenty-four frames per second in front of a projector light. If you stop the movement, one still image would be projected. As the projector speed is increased, passing still images begin changing to appear as slow motion images until the correct speed creates a normal moving picture that creates the illusion of life and motion. The frequency of the passing images determines what we see. Looking at one image every two seconds appears as a succession of still images. Looking at ten images every second appears closer to a normal moving image.

If we want to see the flow of service, we must find the frequency at which the service flow becomes visible. It's like adjusting the speed of a projector to match the speed at which a film was shot. This is the resonant frequency of service feedback that produces sustainable behaviors and actions that move your team or business towards the level of service that the customer considers to be Ultimate.

Sound waves, which vibrate molecules of air, are changed to mechanical movement when the frequency of the air molecules resonate with the hairs in the ear causing nerves to create what we hear. If the frequency is too low or too high, we cannot hear the noise. A normal human hearing range is approximately between 40 cycles per second and 18,000 cycles per second.

How often our heart beats determines the rate of our body's blood flow. Too chaotic (irregular), too slow or too fast, and we stop living. The same goes for business. If the frequency of measurements is too chaotic, too infrequent, or in some instances too frequent, individuals or teams become ineffective, or businesses die.

The frequency of measurement that resonates with poor service is often much lower than the frequency associated with Ultimate Service. But there are situations where frequent service measurements cause poor service. Have you ever gone to a very expensive restaurant where too many waiters come by too often asking if you need anything? The annoyance factor can far outweigh the great-tasting food. This kind of too-frequent service will drive away customers quickly.

If you are asked to report monthly on the status of your work, do you check on your status every day? Or do you wait until two days before the end of the month? Your customer (your manager) has a frequency of once a month. As a supplier, you'll want to have a higher frequency in your supporting Service Flow Pull Structure to ensure that monthly service is ultimately served. If service is important to you, the frequency of measurement is higher than your customer's.

Finding a process to deliver Ultimate Service throughout your internal Service Flow Pull Structure and external supply chain is key to ensuring future success. The measurements and frequencies that resonate with Ultimate Service versus the measurements you currently have will change your company's way of doing business. It may be that you only need to change the frequencies of your existing measurements—normal measurements yielding current normal results, versus Ultimate Service measurements yielding Ultimate Results as you head into the future.

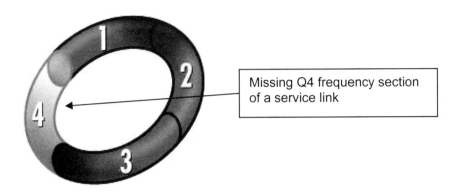

There are three aspects of frequency to consider: one for the convenience of the customer, one for health of the supplier, and one for the quality assurance of the process.

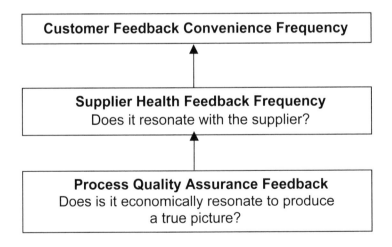

The frequency (rate of measurement) is something that needs to be consciously chosen and then practiced with discipline and regularity. By publishing the frequency, it creates the last important definition on the desired behavior to support the purpose.

When it comes to keeping the level of oil in your car's engine from getting too low, measuring the oil level every time you get gas might be in order—measuring it every minute would be impractical. Older cars measured the heat an engine produced and flashed a light if the motor temperature was too hot. This is an indirect measurement; it does not directly measure the oil level. It could mean the oil level is too low or that something else is causing the motor to overheat. And it's a lagging measure because when the motor gets too hot, the oil level is already too low. This is the classic trial and error process.

The best solution is a gauge that directly measures the oil level and displays it on your dashboard with low and full marks. This way you can see the oil level getting lower as it happens. You can measure the oil level every time you start the car. Before the oil gets to the "very low" mark, you can add oil. This is analogous to waiting for financial measures to signify problems with service. By the time a problem shows up financially, it's already too hot. You need a real-time gauge to prevent the light from ever coming on.

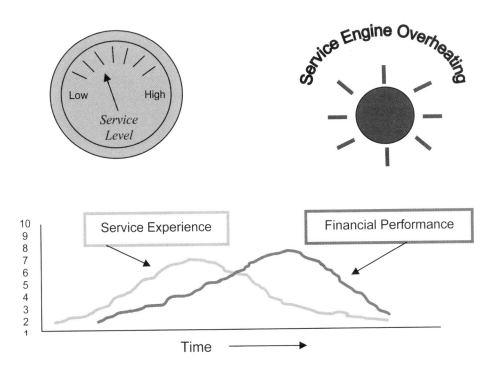

Some kinds of common frequencies:
- Distance — every foot, yard, mile
- Time — every hour, day, week, month
- Event — every rainstorm, fall, football game, election
- Object — every red car, box
- Number– every ten, thousand, million….
- Alphabetical — every name starting with N, with S….
- Customer — every third customer, adult, child, man, woman, team, business

Each process has a natural (resonant) frequency where the measurement supports the purpose for the least cost in time or money.

Frequency can change everything from the outcome created to the sense of accomplishment one receives from creating a service flow. The time span between measurements can be gauged by the amount of time needed to make a correction before it is too late. It is like choosing how long you are willing to wait before knowing that something is going off track, that something is broken, that you are losing money, or that you are losing customers.

There's a saying in the boating world about the best speed for docking a boat: "Approach the dock at the speed you wouldn't mind hitting it." Thinking of that usually makes one move cautiously slow when approaching a dock with an expensive boat.

The opposite could be said when it comes to business: "How fast do you want to know when there is a problem with your service?" This is something you ask yourself, not your customers. But you do need to get a sense of agreement from your customers that the frequency is not too often as to bother them. There is a balance point between asking too often (and being bothersome or intrusive) and not often enough (to prevent poor service).

Our personal frequency for feedback is important to our happiness

How often do you need to know you are being successful? On a personal level, we as individuals are different by design when it comes to the feedback frequency we need for the service we provide in the work we do each day.

Sales professionals that sell long cycle products are different than sales people that sell short cycle products. The long sales cycle of products for a ten billion dollar company might produce only two closed deals in a year. But the salespeople find the needed satisfaction in the process of making the sale itself. The challenge every day is like climbing a mountain: one step at a time resonates with their frequency of reward needs.

Other salespeople that don't like the process but love the closing of a sale would sell similar software products to small businesses. They might close three deals in a week instead of reaching the top of a mountain twice a year. Finding the resonant frequency of success is a key ingredient in finding that "great" job, the one that makes you wonder why you get paid for doing something you enjoy it so much.

A short cycle-of-sale person selling a long-cycle-of-sale product will be frustrated. That frustration will in turn affect the behavior and quality of customer service.

Finding the right job that produces this "joy of work" means finding the unique optimal flow experience for which we are individually designed. This works to feed and strengthen a positive self-awareness, makes us much more productive and open to learning and growing, and results in excellent service.

The opposite case, being in the "wrong" job, is stressful and an impediment to growth. Worse, it results in poor quality service.

Frequency provides a clear picture of flow

Frequency shows us whether or not the flow is what it's supposed to be. Assumptions, fear of the unknown, and energy spent wondering are all affected. The more frequent the measurement, the clearer the view of flow, the more connected we are to the purpose of the flow. In the weight loss example from Step 1, the flow measured is the weight being lost. In the Sales example, it is the flow of cars being sold. In the Production example, there are two flows: the number of TVs coming off the assembly line and the flow of rejects being found.

Example	Flow
Weight Loss	Weight being lost per day
Car Sales	# of cars being sold per week
TV Production	# of TV's produced per day
TV Production	# of rejects per 1000 TV's

Weight Loss
1. What is the purpose? *To reach my ideal weight.*
2. What are the measures of success? *Losing 30 pounds in six months.*
3. What is actually being measured? *The number of pounds and the amount of time.*
4. How often are measurements being taken? *Weighing once per day.*

In this example, the frequency of the weight measurement is once every 24 hours. If the measurements were charted, you could see the process of weight changing. However, if the frequency was once every two hours, there would be fluctuations due to the weight of the flow of food and drink along with changes in actual body weight and would cost too much time. Measuring once a day at the same time would show actual body weight changes without the hour-to-hour variations.

What is the resonant frequency? It depends. For example:

- For those that may get depressed when their weight is not decreasing fast enough, weekly measurements would tend to remove these negative thoughts.
- For those that like seeing any kind of small improvement, daily measurements may bolster their feeling of success and help keep them on track with exercise and diet changes.
- For some that are hospitalized, many weight measures may be performed.
- In some cases, the ultimate weighing frequency may be every hour and may include weighing all bodily input and output to determine if the body's systems are working properly.

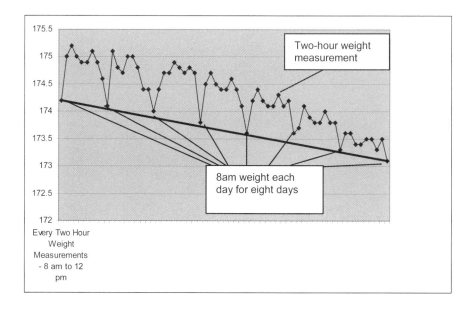

Frequency in car sales

1. What is the purpose? *To increase sales.*
2. What are the measures of success? *Selling 20 more cars each month.*
3. What is actually being measured? *The number of cars sold and the amount of time.*
4. How often are measurements being taken? *Sales reported weekly.*

The frequency of the cars sold measurement is once every seven days. This is the resonant frequency needed for achieving the company's goal—not the customer's frequency. Under this system, car salesmen are driven (pun intended) to push cars onto customers by plying tactics like playing games with pricing or propaganda about the quality and features of the cars.

What if the purpose was changed to: Improve the customer service experience. What would change?

The frequency of car sales would increase, because those customers that avoid doing business with "pushy" car salesmen would return once the new purpose was communicated in advertising and marketing. The Saturn Auto Company car sales process is a good example of how putting service first results in increased car sales and a great reputation. Other auto sales businesses have begun to follow a service-first culture measuring success at the high frequency of each customer.

Frequency in TV production

1. What is the purpose? *To increase the production and improve the quality of the product.*
2. What are the measures of success? *Producing fifty more TVs a month with no more than one defect per 1,000.*
3. What is actually being measured? *The number of TVs produced and the number of defects for every 1,000 TVs.*
4. How often are measurements being taken? *There are <u>daily</u> reports of TVs coming off the assembly lines and hourly reports of the number of defects.*

The frequency of TVs produced is once every 24 hours. Is that really the frequency demanded by their customers? Probably not, but, it *is* the production team's or the company's desired resonant frequency. Looking at how many times an hour a TV is <u>actually purchased</u> would be better. More specifically, how many times an hour is a particular brand and model TV purchased? Matching the frequency of the production rate to the frequency of purchases is one of the goals of lean manufacturing. This measurement is called "linearity." Linearity is intended to be the resonant production rate desired by the customer.

Producing more TVs per hour than customers purchase per hour means that the excess TVs must be stored in a warehouse. Storage is not what customers' request and it adds cost to the production and distribution of the product—costs the customer must absorb. But since manufacturers don't know the resonant frequency, they often produce excess TVs in order to ensure that they always have one on the shelf when the customer comes in to buy.

Storage costs money and adds no value for the customer. The goal of a lean enterprise is to reduce and eliminate all non-value added costs whenever possible. *Lean means having no excess costs, which is one of the results of Pull Thinking and the process of achieving Ultimate Service Flow.*

Set your business' frequency to match the frequency demanded by customers

How do you find the resonant frequency? By communicating and getting agreement with the customer. The Japanese use what is called a Kanban system. The word *Kanban* means signal. Basically, when a customer takes a product off the shelf, a card containing the product model number is given to the supplier to signal a request to make another product to fill the empty space caused by the customer purchase. This process is passed throughout all the suppliers of parts creating a supply chain linked by the communication of Kanban signals. There is no reason to produce anything until the customer purchases a product.

There are mathematical methods used to calculate the frequency of production (production rate) for a production line. The name for the frequency of customer demand is called "takt time." Takt time is a common concept in the field of Lean Manufacturing.

Since the frequency of customer demands fluctuates, production lines are designed for a maximum and minimum rate per day and manned based on the current customer demand rate. This is how lean manufacturing methods resonate Ultimate Service and produce products with extremely low or, in some cases, no inventory.

One of the best resources for understanding these mathematical calculations can be found in the book *The Quantum Leap* by John Costanza. John Costanza is the father of the patented mathematically based Demand Flow® Technology (DFT). His book defines the DFT business, design, and manufacturing techniques and compares them to traditional functional manufacturing. It is a blueprint on how to become more competitive in the global marketplace and grow into the Twenty-first Century.

The number of defects measurement frequency is once each hour

This is another measurement of excess cost. Problems cost customers time and money. They cost the business in repair costs as well as in the costs of preventing problems. Obviously, quality problems cost money and customers expect no problems. This can be summarized as the Cost of Quality.

In the statistical world, a Six Sigma quality level represents a measurement frequency of 3.4 problems out of every million opportunities. This is a very low frequency of problem occurrence. Resonance is demanded to achieve that resultant frequency. Without behavior changes, very robust processes, and prevention techniques, a business must check every product with the ultimate highest frequency of 100 percent, and the costs would be astronomical. Six Sigma quality is achieved by resonating with Ultimate Service throughout an organization. The more robust the process and resultant high quality service, the lower the frequency and cost of measurement.

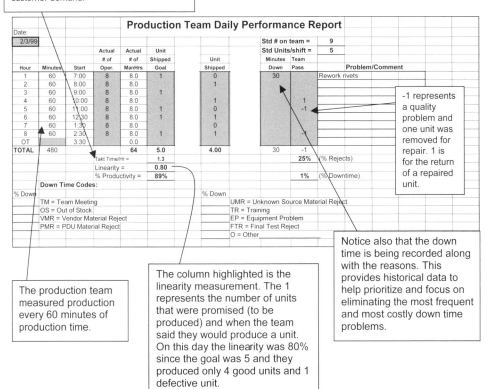

The Takt Time (or production frequency in terms of units per hour) was 1.3 units per hour. This is the resonant frequency of the customer demand.

-1 represents a quality problem and one unit was removed for repair. 1 is for the return of a repaired unit.

The production team measured production every 60 minutes of production time.

The column highlighted is the linearity measurement. The 1 represents the number of units that were promised (to be produced) and when the team said they would produce a unit. On this day the linearity was 80% since the goal was 5 and they produced only 4 good units and 1 defective unit.

Notice also that the down time is being recorded along with the reasons. This provides historical data to help prioritize and focus on eliminating the most frequent and most costly down time problems.

This is an actual production report from a world-class production team using Demand Flow® Technology. The data was hand written in magic marker on a prominently displayed flip chart in the production area by the team members as the workday progressed. It was later typed into a computer to produce the report shown here.

The production would stop and a team meeting would be held if a quality problem arose that was serious enough to warrant it. Otherwise, action items for improvement in the process were discussed at the beginning of each day in stand up meetings. Improvement projects were tracked on a second flip chart. Each improvement idea was tracked daily and included a "who's responsible" column and a "when action is to be completed" column. This gave the team a sense of empowerment, because they could see action being taken and improvements taking place. You could say that daily was the resonant frequency of empowerment.

The daily production meetings were also used to set the production rate for the day based on the actual customer need. This usually meant that the number of team members needed on the production line would fluctuate. If only six out of fourteen team members were needed that day, the other eight team members would be loaned out to other production teams, or they would perform preventive maintenance on equipment, or they would receive cross training. Being cross-trained in all team functions allows each team member to fill in or assist when needed.

This is called "flexing" up or down the production flow to balance out the workloads (even the service flow) when needed.

Solicit feedback proactively

By soliciting feedback and measuring service proactively, you can ensure Ultimate Service. Here are examples of proactive frequency of measurement generators:

- A county Office of Topography Maps asks *every resident* requesting a map to fill out a ten-question quality-of-service form.
- A restaurant chef *visits each table* in the restaurant *once each night*.
- Every *100th customer* receipt has a phone number printed on it to call in order to receive a free dinner in return for answering twenty questions regarding service received that evening.

- A luxury auto dealer calls *every third customer* receiving service and asks four questions about service received.
- *Monthly* project status reports are generated to measure progress.

Examples of non-proactive frequency of measurement generators:

- A monthly financial report (It is an after-the-fact measurement frequency.)
- Comment cards left in a stack on the counter instead of being given to each customer (This is a too-passive effort that is easy to ignore and is often perceived by the customer as meaningless.)
- Complaint box on the wall (This requires too much effort on the part of the customer.)
- A complaint phone number or department (As in the example above, the customer is likely to decide that complaining takes too much effort and will instead take their business elsewhere.)

What do you do with all those feedback forms and data?

- Use data for statistical analysis.
- Group customers based on their similar or different service experiences to see what's working and what's not working in your service delivery.
- Summarize results and publish graphs, charts, and reports, for your team and customers to see. Use the data to measure individual and team performance.
- Look for errors and make sure the customers understand the questions.
- Check to see that your internal measurements predict what your external customer's measurements say. This is covered in more detail in Step 7.

Examples showing the importance of finding the resonant frequency

A Whole Foods Market store posts all customers requests and comments on a public bulletin board for all employees—as well as customers—to see. The store also responds to each of the comments with a hand written response on the bottom of the comment card so that everyone can see it.

Frequency and timing are only part of the measurement process. A second ingredient to frequency is the form in which the communication travels—comment cards, conversations, phone calls, observations, and survey forms, for example. Internal customer measurement processes mostly occur during conversations as we look for nonverbal signals, listen to tone of voice, or simply hear the answers about your service.

Comment cards and survey forms are dictated by the number of customers you have and are usually used just for external customers. However, there is no hard rule about this. Sometimes, in order to get true answers without embarrassing a coworker, internal comment cards and survey forms work just fine on quarterly or annual measurements. Again, ask your customers what works best for them.

In manufacturing, Kanban cards are used to communicate customer demand throughout a business supply chain. Kanban cards (or other methods of signaling) simply represent customer requests for products. They are used as physical symbols to make the frequency of customer requests visible for suppliers taking the guess work out of scheduling.

The words used in proactively asking for feedback are a third ingredient that influences frequency. Your request for feedback form needs to tell your customer that providing feedback is going to genuinely improve their service or sustain their current great service experience. Frequency of response is directly influenced by these words. Waiting for feedback as opposed to seeking it out usually results in a higher frequency of negative comments. Being proactive and seeking out feedback can bring both negative and positive

feedback with a frequency in tune with the service experience. Here
are some good examples:

Dear Customer,

Our primary objective is to take care of you, our valued customer.
We take pride in our ability to serve you quickly and courteously,
with superior quality and at a reasonable price. If you wish to make
any comments or suggestions, or if for any reason we have not lived
up to our high standard of service, please let us know. Your feedback
will help us serve you better.

Please fill out this form and send it to me, or telephone our Customer Service Hotline at 1-800-743-COPY. Hotline hours are 6 a.m.
to Midnight, PST, Monday through Friday.
Thank you.

G. Todd Johnson
President, T.J. Kinko's

♻ Printed on recycled paper.   Tear here

You are a valued customer.
What you have to say is important to us. Please take a moment to
let us know how we are doing by filling out this form or calling
the Customer Service Hotline a 1-800-743-COPY.

This language is slanted
towards wanting feedback if
there is a problem. Wanting
to know if Ultimate Service
was experienced is not
discussed. They are
assuming that no complaint
means Ultimate Service or
maybe just normal service.
There would be no way to
know the level of service
with this language. This is
communicated in the
measurement points on the
form but language here can
help increase the frequency
of positive feedback. The
language in the form below
does call for positive
feedback.

I'm doing my best to be a star in your eyes and make you
100% satisfied with your stay. If you catch me doing
something really terrific—something that meets your needs
in a special way or exceeds your expectations, please fill
out this **CATCH ME AT MY BEST** card. Turn the card in at the front
desk and I'll know you caught me at my best. Thanks.

Dear General Manager,

I caught _____
doing his/her best to make me 100% satisfied with my stay.

(Explanation) _____

100%
SATISFACTION
GUARANTEE

We guarantee high quality accommodations, friendly and efficient service, and clean, comfortable surroundings.

If you're not completely satisfied, we don't expect you to pay.

"It's no problem... just give us a call."

At Hampton Inn, we do our best to make your stay everything you hope it will be. So if you need anything, or should you find something to your dissatisfaction, please call the front desk and let us know. Everyone on the Hampton Inn team has the power to ensure your satisfaction. That's how serious we are about our 100% satisfaction guarantee.

We know you expect the best from Hampton Inn, and we want to make sure you get it!

Nicole

General Manager

P.S. If you prefer, jot down your thoughts on the back of this card and drop it off at the desk.

DAYS INNS OF AMERICA, INC.
339 Jefferson Road
Parsippany, New Jersey 07054

Dear Valued Days Inn Guest:

With all of the choices you have in lodging today, we are honored that you have elected Days Inn for your personal accommodation needs. As our guest, you are our number one priority and we are committed to assuring a pleasant and enjoyable stay.

For over 25 years, you have come to depend on Days Inn for clean, consistent, secure, modern and friendly hotels that meet or exceed your expectations. Whether you are on business or leisure travel, our goal is to continuously live up to your expectations.

We have never made decisions in a vacuum as it relates to exceptional service. We have always listened to you ,our guest, and have used many of your suggestions to improve services, amenities and added value in our product.

This card is provided for just that reason. Please take a few moments to answer these questions and drop it off at the front desk or mail it at your convenience. Your feedback is reviewed by our guest service center and by the management of this Days Inn.

The Days Inn team around the world would like to thank you for your continued support of our hotels. I would like to personally express my gratitude for your business and look forward to hearing from you, my number one priority.

Yours in Hospitality,

Joseph R. Kane, CHA
President and Chief Operating Officer
DAYS INNS OF AMERICA, INC.

REV. 6/96

This describes in detail what expectations they strive to serve and want to know if there are more expectations that they need to know about. The customer frequency of response of expectations will be positively influenced with this language.

Good bold and simple request

Just 'thoughts' are wanted, both positive and negative.

We want your **Feedback!**

Please take a few moments to give us your thoughts on the following:

Type of service provided: *Car sale*   *Service*   *Parts*   *Rental*

Quality of service provided: *Excellent*   *Average*   *Poor*

Timeliness of service provided: *Excellent*   *Average*   *Poor*

Helpfulness of staff: *Excellent*   *Average*   *Poor*

Overall level of satisfaction: *Excellent*   *Average*   *Poor*

Other comments:

Name _____ Phone Number_____

Please phone, fax, or e-mail your remarks.

We value your comments on how we can improve our services to you!

As an incentive, we will have a drawing every month for a $50 American Express Gift Certificate.

Thanks for your help.

This $50 gift offer can certainly influence the frequency of feedback.

It's very important to pay attention to your customer's frequency of measurement. As a supplier, you generally need to measure at a higher frequency than your customer to ensure you're meeting their requirements. Although in the restaurant business, your customer is measuring with each bite, or each new food—but you obviously can't check on them at that rate.

Comments on the Wood Company example from the previous steps:

	Question 2	Question 4	
Action	**Success is:**	**Frequency**	
Provide	100 pcs. of Oak,	Every 2 days	How often the customer needs 100 pcs. of wood.
Cut	12" long,	Every 10th Cut	How often the wood cutter needs to check wood cut against a guage to dimension prevent drift.
Cut	6" wide,	Every 10th Cut	How often the wood cutter needs to check wood cut against a guage to prevent dimension drift.
Paint	painted dark blue,	Every 10th Pc	How often the painter needs to check color against a color chart to prevent color drift.
Pack	loosely packed in a box,	Every Box	How often the packer needs to use a gauge to check packing tightness.
Deliver	delivered every 2 days,	Every 2 days	How often the customer needs 100 pcs. of wood.
Receive	received every 2 days.	Every 2 days	How often the customer needs 100 pcs. of wood.

		Question 2	Question 3			Question 4	
Action	Success is:	What to Measure	Type of Measure	Frequency	Who is the Customer	Who's responsible? (The requester of measurement.)
Provide	100 pcs. of Oak,	#pcs. of wood	Direct, Objective	Every 2 days	Internal Customer C	External Supplier D
Cut	12" long,	# of Feet of Length	Direct, Objective	Every 10th Cut	Internal Customer C	External Supplier D
Cut	6" wide,	# Inches of Width	Direct, Objective	Every 10th Cut	Internal Customer C	External Supplier D
Paint	painted dark blue,	Color	Direct, Subjective	Every 10th Pc	Internal Customer B	Internal Supplier C
Pack	loosely packed in a box,	Tightness of Pack	Direct, Subjective	Every Box	External Customer A	External Customer Supplier B
Deliver	delivered every 2 days,	If Delivered	Direct, Objective	Everyday 2 days	External Customer A	External Customer Supplier B
Receive	received every 2 days.	If Received	Direct Objective	Everyday 2 days	Public	External Customer A

The Pack and Deliver measurement frequencies are different. Pack is every box and Deliver is every two days. Same customer and supplier. The External customer will only measure every box every two days, but Supplier B chose a higher frequency in order to prevent any defective packed boxes.

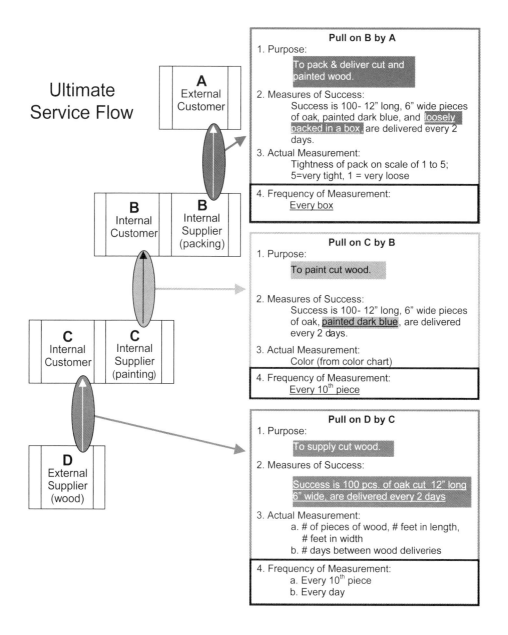

Ultimate Service Flow

A External Customer

B Internal Customer | **B** Internal Supplier (packing)

C Internal Customer | **C** Internal Supplier (painting)

D External Supplier (wood)

Pull on B by A
1. Purpose:
   To pack & deliver cut and painted wood.
2. Measures of Success:
   Success is 100- 12" long, 6" wide pieces of oak, painted dark blue, and loosely packed in a box, are delivered every 2 days.
3. Actual Measurement:
   Tightness of pack on scale of 1 to 5; 5=very tight, 1 = very loose
4. Frequency of Measurement:
   Every box

Pull on C by B
1. Purpose:
   To paint cut wood.
2. Measures of Success:
   Success is 100- 12" long, 6" wide pieces of oak, painted dark blue, are delivered every 2 days.
3. Actual Measurement:
   Color (from color chart)
4. Frequency of Measurement:
   Every 10th piece

Pull on D by C
1. Purpose:
   To supply cut wood.
2. Measures of Success:
   Success is 100 pcs. of oak cut 12" long 6" wide, are delivered every 2 days
3. Actual Measurement:
   a. # of pieces of wood, # feet in length, # feet in width
   b. # days between wood deliveries
4. Frequency of Measurement:
   a. Every 10th piece
   b. Every day

The importance of frequency is the basis for the new science of chaos. Chaos is the science of process and of becoming; traditional science is the science of state and of being. The study of an Ultimate Service process like nature can bring incredible insight and understanding of how to create an Ultimate Service process in business.

Nature's system is a complicated, nonlinear-seeming system of processes. *Frequency enables insight.* Without frequency, all you have is the study of the static state, the present picture. Can you imagine trying to predict the weather based on a single day's measurement? You might be able to tell that it's not raining now, but what does that tell you about whether or not it will rain tomorrow? Even if you could measure all of the contributing factors in a single moment, you couldn't possibly tell how they are changing and moving. For that, you need frequent measures over time.

The science of chaos evolved out of a desire to explain chaotic events in nature. The result of a process caused by a Strange Attractor. It was called "Strange" because there was no other name and "Attractor" because it appeared that the source was a Pull.

Scientists in many different disciplines, including astronomy, physics, and meteorology, continuously looked at the seemingly chaotic movement of natural systems in search of mathematical connections that would predict chaotic movements. To their surprise, scientists not only found connections, but also found that there was a commonality to these connections. Conventional wisdom would think that looking at chaotic events in an organized pattern would still produce chaotic results. The opposite proved true.

Until the frequency of looking at certain chaotic movement was considered (which happened by accident), scientists were unsuccessful in their predictions. Now, Chaos Theory is used to do just that. Science has found the resonant frequency that makes the source of chaos, the "Strange Attractor," visible. Finding the right frequency can show the cause for chaos in business as well.

In business systems, there are many "Attractors," some "Strange" and some not. Those that are not "Strange" are called visions and missions. These are used with integrity that includes the answers to all Four Pull Questions. Within a Service Flow Pull Structure, Chaos in business results from ambiguity and/or a lack of integrity (as discussed in Step 5) regarding the degree of Ultimate Service. The degree is a function of the number of "Strange Attractors" that exist at any given moment in time. Finding and eliminating the strangeness is one of the goals of an Ultimate Service process. This is exactly what successful businesses of the future will do to sustain the process of becoming an Ultimate Service provider.

The fact that everyone's tolerance level is different contributes to Chaos in business. The frequency of complaints about products and services is often dependent upon the severity of a problem that crosses a discomfort threshold and causes the customer to take the time to complain. Below this threshold, the dissonance of poor service may be hidden, unsaid, ruminated upon, or discussed with friends. It might not make it back to the company until a sufficient number of vaguely dissatisfied customers are lost.

Service problems can be uncovered before service dissonance grows by being proactive and asking customers regularly and frequently to comment on their service experience. Chaotic measurements, for example, can result from having the customer comment cards in a holder on the wall where customers randomly notice them. Only those who have gone beyond the complaint threshold would search for a comment card or ask to talk to a manager. It's too late for prevention at that point! Wouldn't it be better to solve the problem before it crosses the customer's threshold?

Again, incenting the customer to respond is the key. This can be as simple as making the customer appreciate that their comments are meaningful and will be responded to or as elaborate as offering discounts and gifts.

An example of how frequency affects what we see is to imagine that you are looking at a swinging pendulum. The pendulum is illuminated by a strobe light tuned to the swing frequency of ten flashes per second. The pendulum appears to be standing still. But as the pendulum slows down while the strobe stays constant at its frequency of ten flashes per second, the pendulum gradually appears to start moving faster and faster from one point to another as if it were jumping.

What you just observed would have been the work of the "Strange Attractor" bringing the pendulum to a stop—Gravity. By increasing the frequency of the light to 100 flashes per second (the light appears to be constantly on) you see a clearly defined swing of the pendulum. The pendulum doesn't appear to be stopping since it is slowing down ever so gradually. But with the higher frequency of observation, you can predict that the pendulum is going to stop after watching it swing through two or three complete arcs.

Finding the right frequency to make the process of slowing down with each swing visible is the key to preventing continued service dissonance or service problems. How often the light comes on is the frequency. How long the light stays on is the measurement. You can take a few measurements at the right frequency and know quickly that there are problems with service, or you can spend a lot of time and money measuring before it is obvious that there is a problem— after which it may be too late to prevent losing customers. It's your choice.

Being able to predict where your service is headed (improving or deteriorating) or where your customer's service flow needs are headed in the future results from measuring at the appropriate frequency. Many things change the customer's needs as time goes on. Is your business designed to resonate with these changes? If not, the pendulum of success will predictably stop. Resonate with your customers to pump energy into your pendulum of success and keep it swinging.

Step 8 deals with going with the flow of change as your customers—your teammates, your team, or your external customers—continue to improve and grow. Being proactive in sensing the sharp bend in the road ahead, changing your DNA, your teams' DNA and your businesses' DNA will be the key to staying in the flow.

Sustaining today's Ultimate Service flow is critical. Planning and rethinking the new purposes and Measures of Success for the changing needs of tomorrow's customers is even more important.

Step 7
Harness the Power of Pull
Taking Action

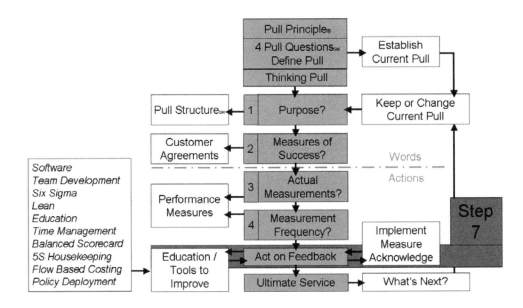

Pull Thinking Process

"Evolution is chaos with feedback."[1]

Pull Thinking is a compass to guide your improvement efforts

Pull Thinking with its tools can become your personal assistant. Barriers become visible and, more importantly, it makes overcoming them easier. Recognizing the barriers to the Ultimate Service Flow helps you understand what other resources are needed. It's as if Jiminy Cricket sat on your shoulder and whispered in your ear. You'll automatically know when you need to learn a new business process, choose a better software package, or find out just who your customers really are and what they think about your service.

At Farberware, Pull Thinking pointed to the need for education to teach hourly workers how to measure their own productivity. They brought in the nearby Bronx Community College to develop a six-week course on subjects like simple math, use of a calculator, English lessons, and team development. The point was to get bigger than the problem, to look at the Service Flow Pull Structure to find where support was lacking. Pull Thinking showed what other resources were needed—in this case it was learning tools.

The following diagrams summarize Steps 3, 4, 5 and 6 into four basic stages in the process of creating Ultimate Service Resonance:

---

[1] James Gleick, *Chaos: Making a New Science*, Penguin Books, 1987

Stage 1: Identify sections of Pulls "floating" around the organization

Stage 2: Organize the sections into Pull links

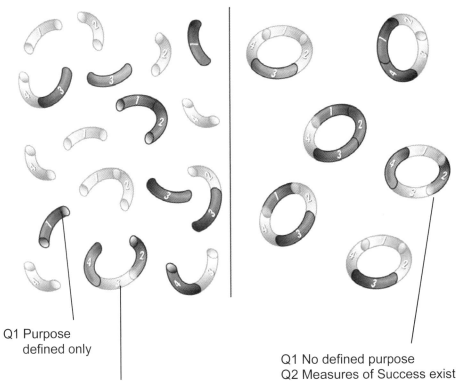

Q1 Purpose
    defined only

Q2 Measures of Success exist
Q3 Measurements exist but no agreement
Q4 Frequency exists & has agreement

Q1 No defined purpose
Q2 Measures of Success exist
Q3 No agreement on measurement
Q4 Frequency exists & has
    agreement

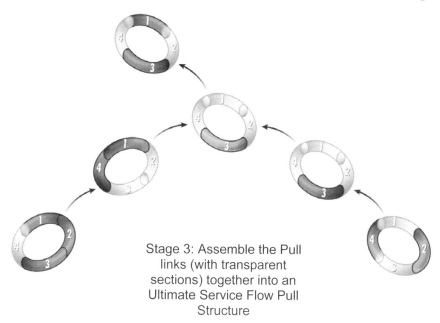

Stage 3: Assemble the Pull links (with transparent sections) together into an Ultimate Service Flow Pull Structure

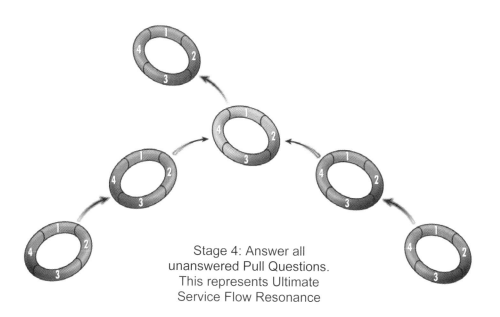

Stage 4: Answer all unanswered Pull Questions. This represents Ultimate Service Flow Resonance

Develop a strategic plan for implementation

Once you've designed an Ultimate Service Flow Pull Structure as in Step 3 (page 91), develop a strategic plan of implementation. First train the executive team on Pull Thinking and then select a pilot area to demonstrate what Pull Thinking looks like with your business's type of service. A typical implementation timeline could vary from 6 weeks to several months depending upon how aggressive you are about change and the need to learn and grow. The form on the following page is from the Pull Thinking Experiential Seminar Workbook and is an example of how people measure their progress during the weeks following the seminar. Measuring the Service Flow Index (as shown on the form) is an excellent measurement on the implementation progress.

It is important in the initial learning process to be active in applying Pull Thinking. Use it or loose it! Using a coach or mentor is an excellent way to ensure that you do not "loose it." In order to ensure that we begin to change how we think about our work and thus change our behavior, the implementation phase must provide time to think about the process, analyze, listen to feedback, and take action to improve (plan it, do it, check it, act on it). Remember, our old way of thinking has been learned over decades of practice. An old thinking voice can sound like:

- There is not enough time; there are already too many other priorities.
- I already do this, why do I need to use this method?
- It's too difficult
- I'm not sure if I'm doing it exactly right

When you hear this, it is time to think about what you want to get accomplished, about the others on your team or in your organization and how a common language like Pull Thinking can help ensure you are all aligned and on purpose everyday. Think in terms of investing the time to learn, to grow and to listen to that other voice is saying: "I want to be successful; I want to know more."

Name: _____ Date: _____ Week: 1, 2, 3, 4, 5, 6, 7, 8, ___

(Week)	1	2	3	4	5	6	7	8
Structure	**Pull Form**	**Meas. form**		**Issues**	**Actions**	**Comments**	**Needs**	**Overall Status**
P								
R								

P = Project or Problem Solving with PT, **R** = Role in the organization's service flow structure. Service flow tied to performance measures.

1. Structure: _____

2. Pull Forms: # of Pull Question Forms complete with agreement _____ (A)
   Total # of Pull Question Forms in your Service Flow Structure _____ (B)
   Your Service Flow Index (SFI) is _____ % (A) / (B) x 100% = SFI

3. Measurement Forms: Have the primary Pull Question Forms been developed? _____
   Are measurements being taken? _____ Are the results published and visible? _____

4. Issues: _____

5. Actions: _____

6. Comments: _____

7. Needs: _____

8. Status: _____ **S**tuck, **Y**ellow (going too slow), **G**reen (progressing well), **C**ompleted

Pull Thinking Implementation Progress Tracking Form

You gain wisdom from what you measure

Look around. What's being measured right now? What are the different ways the measurements appear? Reports being generated are measurements. Are the reports tied to the appropriate purposes serving the appropriate customers? What type of measurements are they: indirect, direct?

If 90 percent of your decisions are Pulled by financial measurements and reports, you need to add an equal weight to customer service focused measurements to bring balance—not in terms of the number of reports, but in the weight they carry in influencing choices.

You could spend four hours on a month-end financial report and five minutes on a customer service report. The time doesn't matter. But the customer service report *must* carry an equal—if not greater—weight as the primary buck-stops-here decision-making source.

Who is doing the measurements? The answer is pretty simple. Just ask one more question. Who is closest to the customer? Who needs to know in order to take action? Those closest to the customer really need to measure—and be responsible for taking action.

Are financial reports being used as lagging measurements on your service? Are the costs being incurred from your suppliers too high because your supplier has poor business systems or poor quality products? Do you increase what you charge your customers? That's probably not the best idea if you want to keep your customers. So instead, do you change to a better supplier or help your supplier improve?

Take this same thought and apply it to internal service and costs. Are the internal services, like record keeping or equipment repair, slow to respond or sloppy in their work? If there are no other choices for the service, use Pull Thinking and *turn complaints into requests*—people can enroll in a request but not in a complaint. Find and list all your complaints, the barriers to Ultimate Service. What requests would eliminate the complaints?

Complaints are a waste of energy and time. They produce stress. Requests reduce the ambiguity of an unknown solution by creating a

Pull—a mission to accomplish when all Four Pull Questions are answered. Everyone wins.

Change your culture – change your business

Changing your business culture may seem like a daunting project. But remember the old adage: How do you eat an elephant? One bite at a time. The same is also true for your business. Start with a first step. Learn from pilot projects. Find just what measures are needed to change and develop a plan of implementing Pull Thinking. Adding the measures on Pull and the Service Flow Index will fundamentally change your organization's culture. Why? Because these measures produce a positive effect on people's behaviors and mindsets regarding all the other measurements that shape your organization's service experience.

This book won't try to give you a recipe or cookie cutter methodology. That would be impossible. All businesses, even those in the same industry, are unique. Using Pull Thinking in your individual business must be customized to its unique needs, as well as for the different levels within it. This book is designed to be a resource for shaping your own cookies.

Go on a "safari" to see how Measures of Success appear throughout your organization

Recognize people's addiction to well-known thought processes and behaviors developed in the environment you have now. See the Measures of Success and measurements that currently exist—policy statements, value statements, rules and regulations, and various reports.

Listen for Measures of Success in every conversation. Thinking of the listener/speaker relationship as a customer/supplier relationship in a conversation can be a strange experience.

But listening for Measures of Success in what others say can be a great influence on your listening quality. Putting communication into categories like "feedback measurements" or "Measures of

Success," or "complaints," or "requests," or "for entertainment only" also aids in applying the Pull Thinking tools.

The process of reorienting oneself takes time and perseverance. The quicker you create visible measurements and self-responsible teammates, the faster and easier changes will be. This reorientation process will be even easier to recognize when Pull is in the air.

So get started. Solve a few problems and get the feel of using the tools.

What about existing projects?

You'll want to take an inventory of all the many improvement initiatives and projects already underway, as well as those that are being planned. Sometimes, companies will have more than twenty simultaneous initiatives in one area!

A Project Priority Grid can be helpful in prioritizing all improvement projects and initiatives according to their direct and indirect influence on key metrics. In the following grid example, "I" represents indirect influence and "D" represents a direct influence on improving service. Key metrics are listed across the top. Each project has a purpose and needs all Four Pull Questions answered. The first column shows which questions need to be answered for each project.

Project Priority Grid

D = Project has Direct Affect
I = Project has Indirectl Affect

Are The Four Pull Questions answered?	PROJECT	RESPONSIBILITY	PRIORITY	EXT CUST SVC METRIC 1	EXT CUST SVC METRIC 2	EXT CUST SVC METRIC 3	EXT CUST SVC METRIC 4	INT CUST SVC METRIC 1	INT CUST SVC METRIC 2	INT CUST SVC METRIC 3	INT CUST SVC METRIC 4	EMP G&D METRIC 1	EMP G&D METRIC 2	EMP G&D METRIC 3	EMP G&D METRIC 4	FIN HEALTH METRIC 1	FIN HEALTH METRIC 2	FIN HEALTH METRIC 3	FIN HEALTH METRIC 4
1,2,3,4	A	Team xyz	TOP		D			D	D						I		D		
1,2,3	B		HIGH			D				D			D			D			
1,2	C	John Smith	HIGH	D					D					I				I	
1,2,3,4	D		HIGH			I						D							I
1,2	E	Jane Doe	HIGH		D						I					D			
3,4	F	Acconting Dept.	MEDIUM						D										I
1, 3	G		MEDIUM			I								I					
1,2,3,4	H		MEDIUM		D														
1,	I	Engineering Dept.	MEDIUM					I						D					D
3,	J		MEDIUM						D										
1, 3	K		LOW		I														I
1,2	L	Plant Services	LOW							I									
1,2,3	M		LOW															I	
1,	N	Executive Team	LOW	I				I				I							
1,2	O		DROP																
1,	P	Jane Doe	DROP																

Personal performance improvement planning is a low-risk do-it-yourself application for Pull Thinking

Create a "safe environment" for change with participation resulting in personal performance improvement planning.

The annual performance review process is probably one of the easiest and highest leverage areas for the investment. First of all, the common frequency of "once a year" is woefully inadequate for Ultimate Service. Increase the frequency on performance measurement. Team members will do their own self-measurement on some of the most important commitment points at higher frequency levels. Yes, that's right. Success based on *commitments* rather than activities. Make sure that the activity points are replaced with customer service commitments. For example: Improving from "good" to "excellent" in accuracy on reports every month instead of merely accomplishing the activity of producing those reports. Are the reports in the best format? Do they contain the most pertinent information that the customer wants? If so, customer feedback becomes one of the main *direct* self-measurements, replacing a manager's *indirect* service performance measurements.

Check out the Service Flow Pull Structure to see which of the Four Pull Questions are missing answers.

The important point is to choose to be heading towards Ultimate Service.

Use Pull Thinking to communicate progress to everyone

Remember, with Pull Thinking, real communication is written. Develop communication systems for everyone in your business, so that everyone, including your customers and suppliers, are aware of progress. Everyone in your service supply chain needs to be in the communication system. Don't underestimate the impact of visual displays of the measurements. Visible measures ensure integrity. Use storyboards showing the various team activities and the results realized. Show photos of the team members with their improvements displayed. Show the education and training needed or planned and the education currently in progress.

Effective storyboards include:

- Detailed Service Flow Pull Structures
  - Team and individual vision and mission statements
    - Measures of Success
    - Measurement results
    - Names of customers
    - Names of suppliers
- Projects underway showing connection to improving the service flow
- Rewards and acknowledgements given to teams and individuals

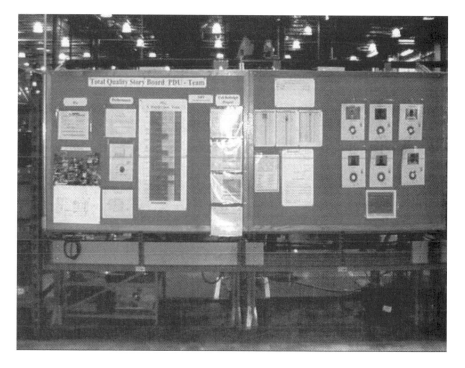

These are examples of company-wide visual displays. Above is the storyboard of one fifteen-member production team. On the next page is a company wide summary of all the initiatives involved in creating a Total Quality (Ultimate Service) Environment. This includes all projects, the status of each, connections to improving service, and responsible project teams, education programs, financial reports, and customer service reports.

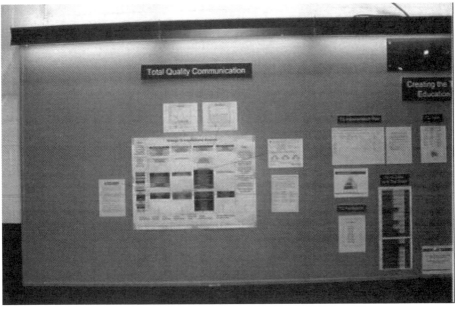

LEFT HALF

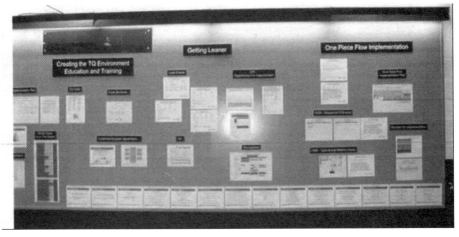

RIGHT HALF

The photo above is from a retail business. Their customer comments on service and suggestions for improvements along with the responses from the business are displayed for all to see. Customers want to contribute when they see that their comments are taken seriously.

The photo on the next page is an example of a large Service Flow Pull Structure on the wall of a large company. The Service Flow Index is changed over time as more and purposes have all four pull questions answered and become Pulls.

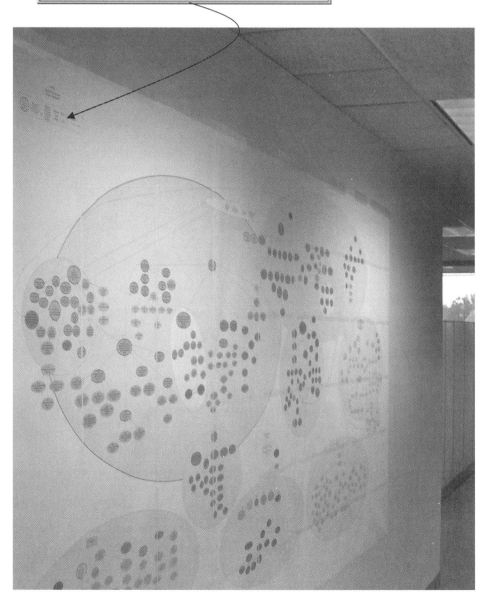

Service Flow Index

48 Pulls/135 Purposes
36%

The following photos were taken at a Goodwill Industries donation facility showing their customer satisfaction.

Find meaningful and personal ways to give rewards and acknowledgement

When Pull Thinking takes off, great things will happen. You'll want to reinforce the positive with rewards and acknowledgements. While this can be done with direct monetary rewards, it is more powerful and generally even more meaningful to use other methods. Below is a list of suggestions:

- Time off
- An acknowledgement lunch
- Public acknowledgment ("Good Job")
- Advancement
- More responsibility
- Added vacation time
- Recognize team of the week or month
- Posting a copy of customer evaluation sheet
- Awards (T-shirts, coffee mugs, etc.)
- Team of the month
- Weekend trip
- Memos recognizing accomplishment
- Preferred parking

Choose the appropriate next step and *go for it!*

Generate lots of Pull Thinking implementation examples, run pilots, and grow. With Pull Thinking, it will be easy to be creative, and come up with your own list. As food for thought, here are some ideas for next step projects:

- Choose a single process to refine
- Initiate a 5S[2] program and get organized (a good place to begin)

---

[2] 5S, abbreviated from the Japanese words Seiri, Seiton, Seison, Seiketsu, and Shitsuke, are simple but effective methods to organize. The 5S, translated into English are: housekeeping, organization, cleanup, keep cleanliness, and discipline.

- Use Pull Thinking to transform a complaints to requests
- Tie Measures of Success commitments to performance measures
- Create a Service Flow Pull Structure to support strategic planning
- Identify resource needs—books, training, team development, Six Sigma, Lean, etc.
- Train your organization first, then introduce Pull Thinking to customers and suppliers
- Look at the environment before and after, and document it
- Change job titles from 'manager' or 'director' to 'coach' or 'facilitator.'
- Learn from other companies with outstanding service like UPS or Ritz Carlton for example.
- Conduct focus groups using both internal and external customers
- Improve communication throughout your supply chain

Put money in its place—as an acknowledgement of service

As discussed in the previous steps, money and financial matters apply to the acknowledgement aspect of Pull Thinking. Just as suppliers ask their customers about their Measures of Success, customers must ask their suppliers about the appropriate acknowledgements for providing Ultimate Service. For external customers, the highest percentage will be financial, while for internal customers a lower percentage will be financial.

Bonus systems for rewarding service above and beyond normal service levels covered by a paycheck have an inherent danger of becoming a barrier to Ultimate Service. If it is done, it should always be given to a team and not to any individual. Reward the behaviors that are consistent with a Pull environment. Since Ultimate Service is a team effort, then team services need to be acknowledged and rewarded—not individuals.

With Pull Thinking, profit, price, and costs are looked at differently. The table on the facing page reveals some basic differences:

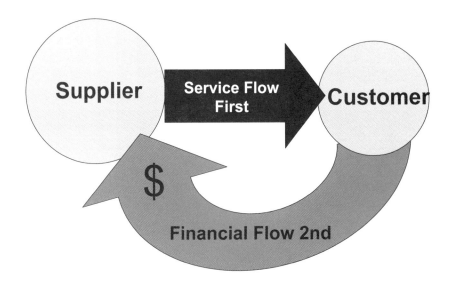

Financial Perspectives

Push Environment

- Primary focus is on near-term profits
  - Focus on incremental cost reductions unconnected with the big picture / supply chain side effects
  - It is OK for the customer to pay for non-value adding work i.e. storage, delays, transportation and inspection
  - Price increased to ensure profit

- Overhead spread over all products equally

- Delays, transportation, inspection are seen as normal operating overhead expense
- Excess inventory is needed to provide products when the customer wants them

- Financial reporting and responsibility is in the hands of top management
- The business is seen as a collection of assets

- IT systems chosen based on financial reporting.

- Fragmented and complex reports as requested by management

- Financial reporting is private

- Cost + Profit = Price (supplier sets price)

Pull Environment

- Primary purpose is service
  - Service includes reducing costs like waste / non-value activities
  - Waste means adding cost without adding value
  - Value means performing work that the customer is willing to pay for
  - Service and costs looked at as entire supply chain – the biggest picture

- Overhead distributed fairly to each product i.e. Activity / Flow Based Costing

- Delays, transportation, inspection are seen as cost adding
- Process is designed to provide customers products on time without excess inventory

- Financial reporting and responsibility given to teams
- Business is seen as a combination of assets and the activities, people & learning needed to extract maximum value from those assets

- IT systems chosen based on integrated reporting needs with equal importance applied to innovation & technology, customer service, people, and financial.

- Integrated and simplicity in reporting as requested by internal and external customers

- Financial reporting is published, transparent

- Price – Cost = Profit (customer sets price)

Money is like oxygen, you can't live without it, but you can get too much of it
— Peter Drucker

Reports provide measurement information for making decisions in business. The measurement reporting generated in a Pull Environment will look different than the reports generated in a Push environment. In his book *Adaptive Enterprise*, Stephan Haeckel describes this difference as decision pull vs. decision push:

"...decision pull means that the decision context establishes the pull signal for information relevant to the decision at hand. Information push characterizes the data glut situation in which one tries to guess in advance what data will prove to be of value."[3]

It's very common that only a small percent of the information in reports you receive will actually be relevant. To make decisions everyday, you and your teammates must pull the exact information you need, no more or no less. You do not need information pushed on you; it ends up eating up your time and diverting your attention. Most software allows report customization, which is helpful if the data you need is already being collected. All too often, that's not the case.

In a Push environment, the decisions made are often based on cost more than quality or delivery. Therefore the data being collected and subsequent reports being generated is financial. In a Pull environment, cost, quality, and delivery, as well as customer

---

[3] Haeckel, Stephan, *Adaptive Enterprise*, HBS Press, 1999

feedback on agreed Measurements (for you as an individual and for your team), would be contained in the reports.

Initially, this may cause you to generate your own reports, using Microsoft Excel or Access, for example. Later, your IT team can adapt your system software.

There are basically four kinds of reports:

- Reports for an internal supplier of service, containing customer feedback on agreed measurements of service points, including quality and delivery

- Reports for an external supplier of service, containing customer feedback on agreed measurements of service points, including quality and delivery

- Reports for the customer of external suppliers containing the cost of acknowledgement, quality and delivery of service experienced

- Reports for the customer of internal suppliers where there may (or may not) be an internal cost of acknowledgement, containing quality and delivery of service being experienced

Create a Pull Thinking Index to measure where you are within the context of the Pull Thinking possibilities

This simple set of questions on the next page serves as a measure on the degree of Pull Thinking implementation—"the Pull Thinking Index." Give your company rating points for each question:

PULL THINKING INDEX

1. To what degree are Purposes, Measures of Success, and Measurements written and results displayed for every team and individual?
    a. 100 percent — 5 points
    b. 75 percent — 4 points
    c. 50 percent — 3 points
    d. 25 percent — 2 points
    e. Pilot only — 1 point
2. To what degree is your Service Flow Pull Structure Index defined?
    a. Entire service supply chain at team level only
        i. 100 percent — 5 points
        ii. 75 percent — 4 points
        iii. 50 percent — 3 points
        iv. 25 percent — 2 points
        v. Pilot team only — 1 point
    b. Entire service supply chain down to the individual
        i. 100 percent — 5 points
        ii. 75 percent — 4 points
        iii. 50 percent — 3 points
        iv. 25 percent — 2 points
        v. 10 percent — 1 point
3. What percent of your associates are fully educated and skilled at Pull Thinking?
    c. 100 percent — 5 points
    d. 75 percent — 4 points
    e. 50 percent — 3 points
    f. 25 percent — 2 points
    g. 10 percent — 1 point

A score of 20 points indicates a 100 percent Pull Thinking environment where all customers are experiencing Ultimate Service Resonance. What is your index?

The same Index questions could be applied to your external

suppliers and used as the basis for deciding between similar suppliers. How many points per month are you increasing?

Display your Service Flow Pull Structure as discussed in Step 3, showing how the index is measured. In the example below, the teams without the answers to all four questions are not colored and have a segment of the line removed to signify which of the questions are missing. The example has the "create bottles" team detailed on the right, showing the individual team members. The team has all Four Pull Questions answered, but four out of eleven of their support suppliers do not. This points to where attention needs to be focused for improvements.

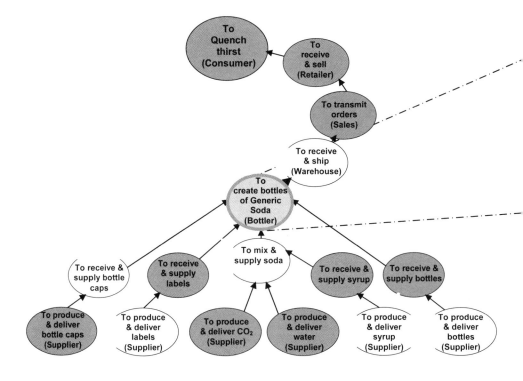

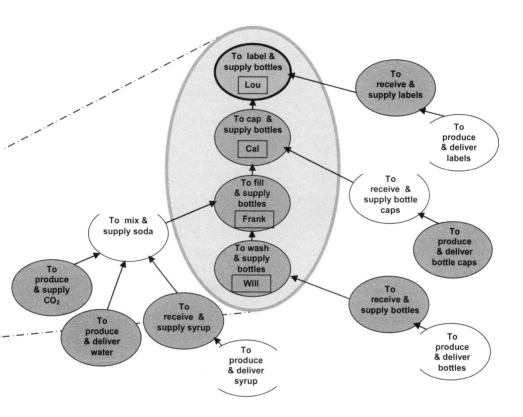

Pull Thinking is simple — but in practice it's not always easy

People's reactions to changing their thinking are complicated. The reactions are different industry to industry, profession to profession, individual to individual. You may never achieve a perfect Pull environment, so there will probably always be some degree of Push to be managed and understood. That's okay. If you can't have a perfect world, settle for making it a consistently better one.

As discussed in Step 2, the desired culture and the resultant environment that supports Ultimate Service is where everyone practices giving improved service through teamwork while utilizing their unique, individual skills. As a result, you will have processes with less wasted time and effort, or less non-value added action.

You'll become embraced in an aggressive way, pulled up to support improved service when and where needed—just in time! A true perspective and strategy will result showing how all of these past big "fad's" or "pushes" relate to the end result of being in the context of Pull. It's like a compass pointing to the appropriate tools right at the exact time they're needed.

Let's take a look at some "real world" examples. The first comes from my own experience.

Anderson Little clothes store example:

An example of a Push changed to a Pull happened when (as an experiment) I worked at Anderson Little years ago, selling suits for a few months. When I sold a suit, the customer often needed alterations. We usually told the customer that his suit would be ready in two to three weeks, depending on how many other customers were in the alteration queue. If you needed your alterations sooner, you *should have* (one of the push phrases) come in sooner for the clothes. For some customers, that was just fine. But for others, the need was more immediate. Maybe they needed a suit for an unexpected job interview, or a funeral, or perhaps a suit had been ruined just before a big meeting. For those people, the Push environment presented a problem. Problems for customers are problems for a business, and ultimately for its employees.

Using Pull Thinking, I came up with an idea. I started by having a conversation with the store manager and asked if we could try a new system. After explaining it to him, he agreed to give it a try.

This is the way the new system was to work:

1. First, I would learn how to shorten a pair of slacks myself, since plain bottoms were very easy to alter and took only about six minutes. Pants with cuffs were more complicated, so they were better left to the seamstresses. If a plain bottom pant was the only alteration needed, the customer would always get his suit before he left the store. There was only a ten percent probability of a correction being needed, meaning further delay.

2. If the suit needed more than slacks altered, I asked the customer when he really needed the suit. Next, I looked at the seamstress's schedule to see if, for example, the following day had time available for the type of alteration needed. If so, I wrote down the customer's alteration, along with the time it would take. The time for alterations was determined and a table was developed to quickly show all salesmen how much time each type of alteration would need. As the suits were sold during the day, the salesmen filled in the seamstresses' schedules—with the customer ultimately determining the completion date.

This system meant that more customers got their suits when they wanted them than before. This resulted in happier customers and more business. I became the number one salesman within a month, beating two other salesmen with more than fifteen years of experience, despite the fact that I'd never sold suits before. Why?

The experienced salesmen chose not to alter slacks. Since no other store offered this degree of service, the store won more business. As an acknowledgement of better service, I attracted more customers, and the manager awarded me a bonus.

I found the customer's Pull by asking: "what is the customers Measure of Success?"

The answer to that question led to identifying the Pull. This new system showed how to resonate with the customer's Pull. Of course, the measurement resonate frequency was every customer. To tell a customer that it will take two weeks to alter a suit for his son when he needs it tomorrow is a Push experience for the customer.

What was the Pull causing that Push? Since the store had no other system, they thought the only way to provide service in line with the Pull of the customer was to take on the additional cost of employing more seamstresses. So the Pull was "to provide alterations at the lowest cost." If one were to include the cost of lost business revenue then adding more seamstresses might be justified given no other system was known. A flow-based cost accounting system, like Activity Based Costing, would make this visible.

However, there *was* another system. I found it by answering the Four Pull Questions.

Another benefit was that fewer suits took up valuable space in the back room. Also, since some customers had only slacks altered and were able to take their suits with them, the salesmen spent less time looking for altered suits when the customers returned to pick them up. That, in turn, meant that there was more time available to be on the floor waiting on new customers.

Implementing Pull

When you begin implementing Pull Thinking, you'll literally be a pioneer in a non-Pull or Push environment. Applying Pull Thinking can be as simple as changing how you listen (keeping the Four Pull Questions in mind), or as complex as planning and problem solving. Here are some accounts of what it felt like during the process of learning Pull Thinking. The first comes from the "inside." Jeff Lebow learned Pull Thinking and decided to join the team.

Jeff's Story

When you first hear about Pull Thinking, it sounds intriguing. You want to know more. It takes some time to absorb the concept and really understand the question. And then there is a moment where it takes hold. You can feel it and know it. It is a feeling of great clarity and energy, because suddenly, you know your purpose, and you have tremendous motivation to pursue it RIGHT NOW! It is hard not to talk about it and think about it all the time, and it can even be a little scary.

Very soon afterward, you reach a state of peacefulness and simply just do it automatically. You listen differently, because you are carefully listening for the answers to the Four Pull Questions. You ask different questions to clarify missing information. When you focus on "what is pulling," it is as if everyone has a description of their Pull force on a sign hanging around their neck — you can see where they're going, easily understand it, and if you choose, know exactly how to support them. You become like "Radar O'Reilly" from M*A*S*H at times—always one step ahead of the need, standing there with the right tool, the right information, the right words at the right time.

Just as a simple example of how Pull Thinking changed my life; time management has always been an issue for me. I've read books and listened to tapes to learn how to get better at it, but soon afterward, reverted to my old habits. Once I got really clear on my purpose, I now had a <u>need</u> to be better at managing my time, and automatically started doing the very things I had learned about but abandoned. This is true in so many areas.

Jeff Lebow
Vice President, Business Development
Alignment at Work, LLC

Kevin's Story

I read the entire Pull Thinking book over Thanksgiving and I was blown away from the book! It has already affected my thinking -- I'm looking at everything I'm doing differently in work & in my life. It's been quite effective so far - on all kinds of things. As a writer, I'm trained to be skeptical, so when something affects me like this, it is the real deal. Pull Thinking is a great metasystem / metatool that makes everything more powerful. There are many things the book states that are common sense and I recognize that taking things to the measurement level isn't commonly done.

In my own life, sometimes I'd leap into things without first defining success. Pull Thinking has given me a way to do this better. Now, before I write an article, I poll some readers to find what they'd want in a story (ask the customer!) and get insight I never would have. This has made my work a lot easier and better. I can now recognize that many successful business leaders I've met with in the last few years are doing Pull but didn't explicitly state it. Now that I see what I'm getting out of it, I'm sorry I put off reading it for so long.

Kevin Howarth
Managing Editor
TechLINKS Magazine

Randy's Story

Recently, I was in a job search mode, and I decided to use Pull Thinking to obtain a job, deliver a new community service, and be a better parent. When I use the 4 Pull Questions to identify and align purpose, it is a credible and very high integrity method of communication. First I ask the other person, and then I share my purpose with them to see if it's a fit. There were times when defining the pull drew a clear line on why we wouldn't be working together. When that happened, there were no winners or losers, just two people who had identified where they didn't have a fit.

Many times during the job search process, I was asked: "Hey, are you interviewing me"? I told them yes. Yes, because we are looking for an alignment of purposes here, and if that's right, then there's more to talk about, if not, then we've simply identified that, and we can move on.

To me, Pull Thinking is a context to deliver a high-integrity message that works well, even with only one person in the group facilitating it.

By the way, as a result of doing this, I got a job for much more money than I ever expected, with a greater title than I was seeking! You better believe I'm going to be using PULL THINKING when I call on my customers, and when I work with my sales staff.

I'll also add that I was never doing any of this with a focus on money. It was always a focus on service. As you can see, the money took care of itself.

I've begun to grasp the power of working with people on their true purpose and checking their alignment with mine. I can't emphasize enough how important this is. It takes some time, but its well worth it. I'm still working on community service and parenting, but I'm already seeing the possibilities for how Pull Thinking can help me in those areas as well.

Thank you,

Randy Randolph
Vice President, National Sales
NewRoads

Donna's story

After using Pull Thinking, managing becomes natural and easier.

Pull Thinking is applying a few not commonly known powerful common sense tools for managing a business. The tools are common sense but they need to be brought to your attention, which is precisely what Pull Thinking does. Pull Thinking includes being instructed on ways to use customer service principles.

Once I attended the Pull Thinking seminar, I was able to apply this thinking to create a strategy for getting these highly intelligent people on my staff to work together for the good of the team. I can't tell you enough about how critically important these principles are to the management of any business.

Donna Calvert
Corporate Operations Manager
Institute of Industrial Engineers

Comments commonly heard after Pull Thinking is initiated:

"My daughter is so excited about work now! What's going on there?"

"I've been looking for something like this for years. It just brings it all together."

"Using the tools of Pull Thinking, we reached agreement on 4 measures without any of the usual resistance and digression. The others didn't even know Pull Thinking and it still worked great."

"The great thing I got out of this is the paradigm shift of motivating people. You can push all you want on some personnel, which will work temporarily, but long term Pull Thinking is the effective way to communicate. I have modified some of my communication techniques with my supervisors, and they are thinking differently. I am seeing improved results…Thank you…"

"We have a brief stand-up meeting every morning to plan what needs to be produced today and how many team members we actually need to be assigned to other teams. We like doing this on our own without a supervisor."

"We are helping each other more now here at Stone Mountain Tool. I'm also using Pull Thinking at home with my son. I just stopped pushing and it's working."

"Creating the Pull Structure helped out a lot and made it easier to understand how we operate."

"Morale is increasing, people are helping each other, and everyone feels more like a member of a team."

These experiences are sometimes similar to what Plato described about the disciples of Socrates experience in *Philebus:*

> *"The young man who has drunk for the first time from that spring is as happy as if he had found a treasure of wisdom; he is positively enraptured. He will pick up any discourse, draw all its ideas together to make them into one, then take them apart and pull them to pieces. He will puzzle first himself, then also others, badger whoever comes near him, young and old, sparing not even his parents, nor anyone who is willing to listen...."*[4]

A vision gives the power to create

A great example of Pull at work is the power that a great vision of purpose can have in creating or turning around an entire business. The power is seen in the activities that occur during the process of pursuing the vision. People aligning their thoughts and activities are in the experience of a Pull environment.

You see this power of vision when a group of employees being called a team are for the first time – through Pull Thinking – learning about being a team and how teams pull together. Their first task is to develop their own vision of their team purpose. In the following example, one team's purpose became:

PDU Team

Vision: We build the best Power Drive Units wordwide.

Mission: To delight our customers by producing Power Drive Units for Cargo systems by doing what we say, with high productivity, excellent quality with no rework and on-time delivery everyday.

Success is that:
Our daily productivity is 90%
Our linearity is 1 everyday – we do what we say we are going to do
Our quality is 100% every day with no team passes
There is 0% rework every day

---

[4] Mihaly Csikszentmihalyi, *Flow: The Psychology of Optimal Experience*, Harper & Row 1990

Thus began their process over the next several months of becoming a world-class team. They helped design their production line and took on the responsibility to daily track their own production performance and their own problem solving. Their context for being at "work" had changed. They were being pioneers for the rest of the 600 employees, learning how to align their thoughts and actions to serve their customer everyday. These pilot team pioneers found out what it takes to be successful at Total Quality service while their surrounding environment stayed the same and were not afraid to tell others. Their team leader was proud to give his accounting of their team building progress to the many groups during the next several months in Total Quality education sessions held. Each class included Pull Thinking as the basis for Total Quality and Lean Manufacturing.

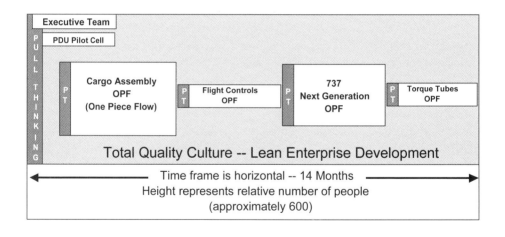

Pull Thinking pulls the individual to creativity and outstanding achievement

Pull Thinking is more than a toolset or a recipe. Pull Thinking is just that—a way of thinking. It connects diverse, and sometimes seemingly random elements into an order, a flow. That's what allows us to view situations around us in creative new ways. It makes every experience more harmonious. In his book *Flow: The Psychology of Optimal Experience*, Mihaly Csikszentmihalyi makes this point:

> *"But to change all existence into a flow experience, it is not sufficient to learn merely how to control moment-by-moment states of consciousness. It is also necessary to have an overall context of goals for the events of everyday life to make sense. If a person moves from one flow activity to another without a connecting order, it will be difficult at the end of one's life to look back on the years past and find meaning in what has happened. To create harmony in whatever one does is the last task that the flow theory presents to those who wish to attain optimal experience; it is a task that involves transforming the entirety of life into a single flow activity, with unified goals that provide constant purpose."[5]*

Perhaps most importantly, Pull Thinking helps us realize our ultimate potential as thinkers, as workers, and as human beings. It shows us how we are connected to all others around us. It shows us how everything—and everyone—relates and interacts.

When we understand Pull, we can contribute more. We can provide Ultimate Service, and we can receive the acknowledgements we crave. That's no small thing—in fact, it's a pretty powerful Pull.

In short, by understanding the flow around us with Pull Thinking, we're more satisfied with our work, our rewards, and our

[5] Csikszentmihalyi, Mihaly, *Flow: The Psychology of Optimal Experience*, Harper & Row, 1990

lives in general.

Csikszentmihalyi knew this, too.

> *"But complexity consists of integration as well as differentiation. The task of the next decades and centuries is to realize this underdeveloped component of the mind. Just as we have learned to separate ourselves from each other and from the environment, we now need to learn how to reunite ourselves with other entities around us without losing our hard-won individuality. The most promising faith for the future might be based on the realization that the entire universe is a system related by common laws and that it makes no sense to impose our dreams and desires on nature without taking them into account. Recognizing the limitations of human will, accepting a cooperative rather than a ruling role in the universe, we should feel the relief of the exile who is finally returning home. The problem of meaning will then be resolved as individual's purpose merges with the universal flow."*[6]

Of course, Csikszentmihalyi's point raises a rather interesting question. On the surface, he seems to be talking about living beings or communities. A business is neither. It's not an organism. It's a tool, a machine. It's merely an instrument created by human beings to be used by human beings, right?

Or is it?

A corporation needs nurture, connection, and sustenance in order to survive. It needs to interact with others—it needs community. It thrives in an environment of flow—from supplier to customer. So perhaps it's appropriate to think of a business as an organism after all.

> *"Is it that we think life starts and ends with us {humans}? Surely, simpler organisms are alive. Why then can't we regard more complex*

---

[6] Csikszentmihalyi, Mihaly, *Flow: The Psychology of Optimal Experience,* Harper & Row, 1990

organisms, like families or societies or companies, as being alive as well? Is the tide pool, a teeming community of life, any less alive than the anemones, mussels or hermit crabs that populate it?"

— Peter Senge

Examples of Pull at work in nature:

Author Richard Koch points out that almost the only class of complex system in the universe that is not purely self-organizing is the modern business corporation and other hierarchical organizations modeled on it. In fact, Koch argues in his book *The Natural Laws of Business*[8] that there are eight benefits in treating the firm as an organism rather than a machine:

1. It takes away the illusion of control. A living thing is more difficult to control than a machine. An organism is unpredictable and headstrong, with a mind of its own.
2. It stresses the role of growth and innovation. Machines don't grow. Organisms can't do anything else or they die.
3. It reminds us that organizations, or parts of them, can be self-starting. A machine needs to be started, switched on and switched off. Machines suffer from entropy: they run down unless they are regularly maintained. Organisms can start themselves and renew themselves; they grow new cells and regulate heir own metabolisms. Whole industries can organize themselves better when central decision-making is removed.
4. Organisms are part of systems. An organism is a complex whole composed of many subsystems and part of many "super-systems" above it. The corporation is going to be affected by a change in its subsystems—for example, by the recruitment or retirement of individuals—and by super-

---

[7] Senge, Peter, *The Fifth Discipline*, Currency Doubleday, 1990
[8] Koch, Richard, The Natural Laws of Business, Currency Doubleday, 2000

systems—its market and competitive environment. Machines are not affected like this.

5. Organisms can build networks and relationships. Machines can't. With networks and relationships, economic progress is easier, faster, and greater.

6. Organisms have their own purpose. Machines have the purpose prescribed by their builders or owners. Organizations have purposes that evolve as a result of their founders' characteristics and what happens along the way.

7. Organisms learn. Only living things can learn. Clearly, organizations can learn. Knowledge exists as a function of working together within the human players, not in the organization independent of its members.

8. Finally, organisms can have their own character and uniqueness. A machine that has its own characteristics rather than those intended by its designers is probably not a very good machine. Humans, and possibly other organisms, have emotions, which lead organizations to have their own cultures that are the product of history and accident as well as human design.

Pull Thinking: The Physics of Business

Through Pull Thinking, you can find direct comparisons and answers to complicated questions by looking at the discoveries of the Science of Chaos. Pull Thinking is like looking into the night with an infrared night-vision scope—the change in frequency makes it all visible.

So what does this have to do with gathering feedback and improving the results? Simple. Organisms in the physical world respond to physical laws. It is the nature of a living organism to give feedback. A baby cries when it's hungry. Plants grow towards the sun. Organisms thrive when their needs are fulfilled. We have a Pull to fulfill and to be fulfilled.

Your customers *want* to give feedback so that you can provide Ultimate Service. It's only natural. You *want* to give your suppliers feedback.

The data is there. All you have to do is measure, and create a new vision in response.

The trick is to listen, to use that feedback. Don't just measure. Change, learn. Measurements shine a light on opportunities for improvement. What do you learn when you see which way a plant grows? That it needs light. Your customers are giving you clues, too. The Four Pull Questions help you read those clues. They help you measure. They ensure that you will improve and provide better – and eventually – Ultimate Service.

Create a vision of Ultimate Service. Develop missions and purposes to achieve it. In short, align your Pulls with those of your customers. Then, measure the results. Use the information to acknowledge and improve.

Corporations are going to have to acknowledge the fact that what they want to create in terms of growth and profit is not necessarily what people are willing to work for in terms of greater meaning and shared purpose. That's a lesson that's starting to creep into our thinking.

Step 8
Ultimate Service – What's Next?

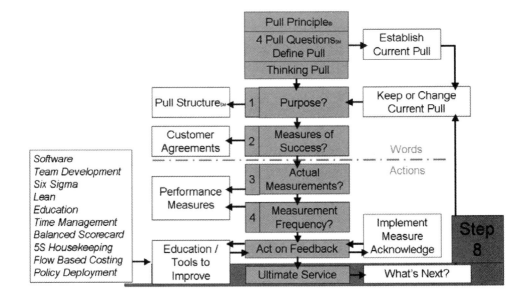

Pull Thinking Process

Something takes place that resembles a whole industry retooling for new production. In the words of Thomas Kuhn, a science historian, "It is rather as if the professional community had been suddenly transported to another planet where familiar objects are seen in a different light and are joined by unfamiliar ones as well."
— James Gleick [9]

What does Ultimate Service look and feel like?

How do you know when you have achieved Ultimate Service? For everyone—every individual, every team, and every business—Ultimate Service will look and feel different. You can't stick in a toothpick to see if your Ultimate Service cake is ready. But you *can* get a fairly good idea of where you stand by using the two Push versus Pull tables presented toward the end of this step. But don't look ahead yet.

In the mean time, here's something to remember. Ultimate Service is about continual improvement. If you think you've finally and forever achieved Ultimate Service, dig deeper. On the other hand, if you think you're constantly improving and getting better and better every day, you may be closer than you think.

Does that mean Ultimate Service is an unobtainable goal? Absolutely not. It *does* mean that Ultimate Service isn't static. If you achieve it today, don't rest and get comfortable. In the process of providing Ultimate Service today, you must stay closely sensitized to your customers so that you sense when their Pull is about to change. Your customers want you in their flow—Pulling with them as their own Pulls change. Thinking Pull, your entire organization will become more agile—able to flow with your customers.

---

[9] James Gleick, *Chaos: Making a New Science*, Penguin Books, 1987

As you progress beyond the initial implementation phase and more teams practice Pull Thinking, your organizations' mindsets and behaviors will be constantly upgraded.

Continuous improvement is going on with your customers

That means Measures of Success will change continuously. Your suppliers will also need to know how your service needs are changing. (See how this works? *Your* needs are changing, too.) Going with the flow, sensing and adapting, is continuous. Changing one person's vision (or creating a vision for the first time in a single employee) is a change in your service supply chain. Teams will go through the same identity changing process—perhaps creating a real identity for the first time ever.

Culture (your business's DNA) is a sum of measures, so changing measures means changing your culture as new technology is delivered and measurement possibilities are improved. Twenty years ago, for example, human DNA matching was not available as a measurement. Today, it is. This has significantly changed our criminal defense system. The Internet has enabled millions of people to access new types of measurement systems—fueling rapid continuous improvement possibilities.

Over time, your mission, goals, and purposes may—and should—change fairly frequently. Your vision, on the other hand, will change less often, because it is a much longer time frame. It all depends on how far reaching or sustaining your vision is. Remember this example from Step 3?

"64K of memory is all anyone needs in their personal computer"	vs.	"Computers with ever-increasing memory"

Fourteen years ago, the vision on the left lasted about six months. The vision on the right will probably go on forever. Of course, this type of vision of service now includes higher speeds, lower cost, smaller and more portable units, attractive design, and much more.

A good vision endures, but purposes evolve. In fact, individual purposes change as one moves on to new assignments in business. But we often deny the need to change our personal purposes and performance measures. Pull Thinking compels us to change.

It also keeps us watching for changes in our own service needs. As a consequence, it also causes us to communicate with our service suppliers. That communication supports their ability to proactively adapt to our changing needs and service flows within the supply chain just as we adapt to our customers' changing needs. Remember, you need to take responsibility to ensure that your suppliers are listening properly. Keep asking questions that measure your service from your teammates or supply teams. The answers will help you make sure you're aware of any changes in their Measures of Success. Having them visible is an important part of ensuring Ultimate Service.

Take care of your service identity — personal, team and external

This is your book cover, how others think of your service. The attractor that Pulls your customers in. But it can also be a detractor, pushing your customers away. Where are you on the charts on the next two pages,? In the left column? Or more in the right column? What do you want your identity to represent?

Push Environment
- Complicated and difficult
  - There are no clear purposes and measures. People create their own internal purposes, causing disagreements
- Primary purpose is profit but not advertised as such
  - That is the classic definition of business. Everyone does it this way. Okay to not have integrity
- Less communication
  - Executives and managers are running the show and employees are on a need-to-know basis only
- Slow communication
  - Bureaucracy and the need to go slow to avoid mistakes; too many measures in hands of a few
- Complaints
  - No other choice, squeaky wheel method works
- Others are responsible
  - Others have the measurements— executives, managers, supervisors
- Managed
  - The belief is that most employees are not capable of becoming self-managed. If that were so, what would a manager's job be?
- Accumulating power
  - The need to climb the ladder of success to achieve the rewards and feeling of power
- Detection
  - Finding problems and fixing them is my job. More recognition than from prevention. Easier to justify financially

Pull Environment
- Simple and easy
  - Purposes and measures are clearly defined with agreement among everyone
- Primary purpose is service
  - People demand integrity and are respectful of what their customers want
- More communication
  - People know that real communication produces growth
- Faster communication
  - To prevent problems faster and speed the growth
  - A few measures in the hands of many
- Requests
  - Requests include purpose, MOS, M. & Freq.
- I am responsible
  - There is participation and agreements on the Four Pull Questions.
- Facilitated
  - Education and resources support feedback via common purposes
- Giving power away
  - No reason to keep power— obviously a barrier to Ultimate Service Flow
- Prevention
  - Barriers become visible earlier, providing opportunity to remove

Push Environment

- Symptoms
  - We are used to this and taught the tools of symptom measurements. Often easier to see symptoms than causes
- Secrets
  - The less you know the more freedom I have. Fear of reprisal if not a secret
- Trial and error (random) improvements
  - Easier to detect and justify financially because of the present method of accounting
- Measures of Success are known <u>after</u> the fact
  - Resulting from trial and error methodology; we were taught and mentored in this method
- Little education
  - We all went to school already, no need to do that again, it was not a good experience
- Broadcasting
  - Mostly speaking and not used to listening; a lot of listening for "what you can do for me" "OK – Let me tell you what I can do for you."
- I know only my part in the "big scheme of things"
  - No service structure exists
- More stress
  - Due to more ambiguity therefore less control
  - I am not in the management communication loop
- Maximizing the utilization of the resources
  - Because financial measures drive us to "being efficient"

Pull Environment

- Causes
  - More people involved asking "why" many more times with support from Service Flow Structure
- Transparent
  - Secrets are now seen as barriers to growth and service improvement
- Continuous improvement
  - Continuous frequent visible measurement Pulls constant improvements.
- Measures of Success are usually known <u>before</u> the fact
  - Agreements naturally require this
- Continuous education
  - Needed to support continuous service improvement and continuous growth
- Listening
  - Listening with the Four Pull Questions in mind and with a customer/supplier awareness, "Tell me what you want me to do for you?"
- Everyone is "on the same page"
  - Service Flow Structure is highly visible
- Less Stress
  - Less ambiguity; therefore more control of work environment with agreed purposes and knowing the connection to the Service Flow Structure
- Maximizing the flow of service to the customer
  - This is why we exist—we continuously get better from continuous feedback

What's next?

Your customers want you to keep from getting comfortable with your current mission and Measures of Success. Remember as you go forward that Push thinking makes us want to *not change*. Pull Thinking compels us to want to continually change, grow and improve.

The Pull Principle is present around us in all we think, do and see. Pull Thinking is natural. It enables us to create our own Ultimate Service flow. It's the right thing to do. Finding out what it looks and feels like in your own unique environment is for you to discover.

"Pull Thinking doesn't need proof — it needs practice."

Appendix A   Pull Thinking® Measurement Form

By now you know how important it is to measure customer service experience. Please take a moment to complete this measurement form.

1 = Not Important / Not Clear   5 = Very Important / Very Clear

Topic	1 - 5	1 - 5	Comments
Pull Principle®			
The Four Pull Questions			
Ultimate Service Flow Pull Structure			
Ultimate Service Flow Index			
Pulling vs. Pushing			
How to Change Culture			
Role of Money			
Identity, Growth and Pull			
Team Pulling Together			
Customer/Supplier Alignment			
Service Resonance			
Who's Responsible			
The Pull Process			
Integrity & Pull			

Pull Thinking

1. Which Steps were difficult?

   Which Steps were easy?

2. Did you use the Four Pull Questions and if so, what was your experience?

3. Has Pull Thinking changed your perception of your environment?

4. What are the three top questions you have about Pull Thinking?

5. Is this something that you would recommend to others?

6. Was the book easy to read?

7. Other comments and suggestion...

Would you give permission to be quoted? _____

May you be contacted? _____

(Optional)

Name _____

Email _____

Phone _____

Please cut out and send to:

Ken Meyer
Alignment at Work, LLC
5555 Glenridge Connector
Atlanta, Georgia 30342-4740

OR:
email: ken@pullthinking.com

THANK YOU!

Appendix B

Pull Thinking Frequently Asked Questions

1. What is the Pull Principle?

- The Pull Principle defines the primary force that causes all action as a Pull force with a Push force being in response to (the result of) a Pull Force.
- The most efficient way to create, grow and improve is to Pull. Pull is a force of nature that no one can avoid or alter.

2. What is the purpose of the Pull Principle?

- It describes the unifying creative force of nature that exists all around us and defines the relationship between push and Pull.
- It provides a common language to enable us to create what we want to create in line with the force of nature.
- It puts a measure on the creative process.

3. What are the Four Pull Questions?

- What is the Purpose?
- What are the Measures of Success regarding the Purpose?
- What is actually being measured?
- What is the frequency with which the measures are being taken?

4. What is the Purpose of the Four Pull Questions?

- The Four Pull Questions define a Pull. By answering them, the Pull becomes visible, enabling one to make better choices in one's actions.

5. What is Pull Thinking?

- You are aware of what is Pulling and use that as a basis of making choices and taking actions based on the Pull Principle.

6. What is the purpose of flow and its relationship to turbulence?

- To identify the barriers (waste) that is inhibiting and reducing service to customers. Pull causes flow, and makes these barriers visible. The barriers pushing against the flow cause turbulence.

7. How do you discover what is really Pulling a project?

- By looking at what is actually being measured.

8. When is pushing appropriate?

- When it improves flow, reduces turbulence, is requested and / or enables the Pull. (Inappropriate push impedes flow, causes turbulence, and reduces the Pull. Pulling includes positive pushing as part of the Pull.) Pulling is improving the flow, causing growth. Negative push impedes growth, and reduces Pull.

9. How do you support flow?

- By improving alignment and removing obstacles.
- By providing a Pull Structure.

10. What is the source of wisdom?

- "The hypothesis has been proposed that if the mind of man is exposed to the economy of nature, as revealed in the workings of living systems, he will become sensitized to recognize the necessity of balancing values. Thus, measure is established as the source of wisdom." -- Jonas Salk

11. What is the purpose of Money?

- To serve as an acknowledgment of service. It is often used as a secondary Measure of Success producing less than the maximum results.

12. When does "Pull" start?

- When the measure starts. (When does the flow start? -- when the Pull starts)

13. What is the purpose of communication and when is communication real?

- Communication provides the connection for measure to occur. The spoken or written word is one kind of communication that connects. Another, used in manufacturing, is the Kanban. Communication is real when it is written or visible.

14. How is customer service related to flow?

- Customer service is aligning the flow of service to the Pull of the customer. Pull Thinking recognizes that most of the supplier / customer relationships are internal.

15. What is the purpose of the structure of an organization and how is Ultimate Service achieved?

- The organizational structure supports growth by ensuring that the flow of all energy (service) is aligned with the purpose of the organization. The ultimate organization structure is a Pull Structure.
- Pull causes the flow of service and the Pull Structure defines the position of the Pulls and shows where the flows of service needs to, or wants to go. It is not necessarily ultimate unless all Four Pull Questions are answered and agreed upon. The process of heading toward Ultimate service can start tomorrow but you may never actually get there especially given the fact that your customers' needs and demands change as time goes on. The important point is to get the structure in place to enable the flow process. This is what is exciting about Pull Thinking; you can start very quickly!

16. How do you know who is responsible?
- The person measuring or requesting the measure.

Appendix C—Glossary

Alignment – internal and external, suppliers and customers have the same answers to The Four Pull Questions. Customer requests become supplier purposes.

Balanced Scorecard—based on a book by Kaplan and Norton, a balanced scorecard is a way for a business to track all of their important performance measurements in addition to financial.

Business—the dictionary definition of business refers generally to the buying and selling of commodities and services and connotes a profit motive as its primary purpose. In Step 2, Pull Thinking defines three types of business activities:

- Business—services you choose to give to customers, (including buying and selling commodities and services), with the primary method of acknowledgement of services being money
- Non-business—services you choose to give to customers, (including buying and selling commodities and services), with the primary method of acknowledgement of services being other than money
- Combination of business and non-business

In all cases, what is common is service; the difference is simply the method of acknowledgment.

Cpk—a good measurement for suppliers to use to ensure all products meet customer specifications or standards which remove the need for customers to inspect supplier's products. Technically speaking: a measurement of dispersion about a specification midpoint and centeredness of a process capability Cp. This is commonly used in a Six-sigma program, and gives an indication of how well the process is capable of meeting the customer specifications. A Cpk of 1.0 indicates that 99.73% of parts produced are within specification limits resulting in about three out of a thousand parts needing to be repaired, scrapped or rejected. The higher the value, the better. Cp, a process capability of achieving the customers requested service specification or standard, usually applied to measurements in manufacturing production. Reference: *DataMyte Handbook*, DataMyte Corporation, 1984, page 5-9, 5-10.

Culture — (DNA) is the collection of measures (values) for an organization. As a rule, when you change the measures, you change the culture.

Customer — the person, team or business receiving service, Pulling the supplier. There are two types in any business — internal and external. The *external* customer is at the top of the business Service Flow Pull Structure, Pulling *internal* suppliers and customers.

Dissonance — the opposite of resonance. "Noise" or resistance in the flow of service that interferes with or diminishes Ultimate Service Flow.

Empowerment — To be empowered is to take on new measures, to empower is to give measures away.

Flow — physical or non-physical movement with a Pull as the source. Ultimate Service flow — see Ultimate Service Flow Pull Structure — see Service Flow Pull Structure

Four Dimensional Alignment — when all Four Pull Questions are agreed upon between customer and supplier. Each Pull question is one dimension on alignment.

Four Pull Questions — one of the three Pull Thinking tools — four questions that when understood and agreed upon between

supplier and customer, define the Pull force from customer to
supplier.

- What is the purpose?
- What are the Measures of Success?
- What are the actual measurements?
- What is the frequency with which the measures are being
  taken?

Frequency of measurement—a technical term to express "how often"
measurements are taken. The 4th Pull Question.

Giving of yourself—taking a risk by going outside of your identity, *I*,
and into the possibility, *P*, to serve others.

Growth—Increasing what you know you know, decreasing what
you don't know you don't know and what you know you don't
know.

Identity *("I")*—"what you know you know," the sum of all your
memories, measures/values and experiences.

Integrity of purpose—all Four Pull Questions aligned to a specific
purpose.

Lagging measurements—lagging measurements are "after the fact"
measurements of results, as opposed to real-time measurements
of service. In most businesses, financial measurements are all
lagging.

Leading measurements—leading measurements are real-time
measurements that are used to detect trends (positive and
negative). An SPC control chart is a leading measurement of
quality, just as real-time customer service measurements will
let you know how your business is serving customers long
before your financial (lagging) measurements will.

Lean and Lean Thinking—a result of Pull Thinking where identification and removal of non-value added actions or waste is reduced or eliminated to reduce costs and improve the flow of service. No waste is lean. Thinking in terms of becoming lean by eliminating non-value activities.

Measurement—quantification of characteristics or behaviors physical or non-physical. Used in the 3rd Pull Question. (What is the actual measurement?) Used in the context of the 2nd Pull Question. (What are the Measures of Success?)

Measures of Success—all the measures and values in regards to a purpose that provide the context in which actual measurements are made. Where you can look to determine what measurements/values to make.

Mental model--that part of our identity containing what we know about service—the images, assumptions and measures regarding service.

Non-business activity—service you choose to give to customers who primarily acknowledge it by means other than money. (See business activity)

Possibility ("P")—a possibility is something you recognize that "you know you don't know." That possibility will cause you to grow and learn, as you give of yourself to pursue it.

Pull— the creative force in nature—a strong Pull has agreement between customer and supplier on all Four Pull Questions. This is also Four Dimensional Alignment. The source of any flow is a Pull.

Pull chain—a methodology for depicting customer/supplier service links arranged in a Service Flow Pull Structure.

Pull environment—an environment where there are visible answers to the Four Pull Questions that are known up-front, or easy to obtain when requested. Where all the tools of Pull Thinking are being used—The Pull Principle, The Four Pull Questions and the Service Flow Pull Structure.

Pull of the *I*—the Pull of the identity, the product of all your personal issues, fears, etc. that has the effect of keeping you inside your self, and unwilling to go outside yourself in pursuit of possibilities. If the Pull of the *I* is greater than the Pull of the possibility, you will "stay inside" and not pursue it.

Pull Principle—the basic tenet of Pull Thinking that explains the relationship and distinction between Push and Pull. It states: "The Primary force that causes all movement is a Pull force; a Push force is in response to a Pull force. The most efficient way to create, grow and improve is to Pull. Pull is the creative force of nature that no one can avoid or alter."

Pull Thinking—thinking and acting based on what is Pulling.
　　-No contradictions
　　-Enhances the other three ways of thinking

Pull Thinking Index—a simple set of questions that serves as a measure on the degree of Pull Thinking implementation.

Pull Structure— a methodology for identifying and creating the relationship between Pull forces necessary to enable the flow of Ultimate Service. (see Service Flow Pull Structure)

Push—a force in opposition and/or in response to a Pull force. It can only exist with a Pull force. By definition, anything that is not "Pull" is "Push." Not having agreement between customer and supplier on one or more of the Four Pull Questions.

Push environment—an environment where the answers to the Four Pull Questions are not visible, do not exist, or are not easy to obtain when requested, or are not agreed upon between supplier and customer.

Request—made by a team member or someone you are aligned with (either customer or supplier). The expectation is that you will execute their request in support of their need. It is what needs to happen to remove a complaint.

Resonance—when *all* of the customers (both internal and external) in the Service Flow Pull Structure are experiencing Ultimate Service.

Responsibility—belongs to the one measuring, requesting the measurements, or valuing. Best if it belongs to the one who needs to know that is closest to the customer who can take action and improve the flow of service.

Service Flow Index—percent of purposes without all Four Pull Questions answered verses all purposes in a Service Flow Pull Structure. Used as a measurement that shows the % possibility of Ultimate Service Flow resonance. Can be used to show the rate of improvement toward reaching Ultimate Service Resonance.

Service Flow Pull Structure—an organizational structure that is unique for every customer, where all of the people (teams/groups) are in the Pull of the external customer. This is measured by having defined Pulls between each piece of the structure. A Service Flow Pull Structure ensures the flow of Ultimate Service to the eternal customer.

Six Sigma—a systematic process for reducing variation and continuously improving. A Six-sigma quality level measurement is commonly defined as a maximum of 3.4 defects per million opportunities.

Supplier—the person, team or business providing service, being Pulled by the customer. There are two types in any business—internal and external. The *external* supplier is at the bottom of the business Service Flow Pull Structure, being Pulled by *internal* customers and internal customers/supplier service flows in support of the external customer.

Trial & Error process—a process where the measures of success are only known after the fact (usually occurs a Push Environment). Trial & error processes are characterized by constant missteps and resulting feedback in pursuit of a specific purpose.

Ultimate Frequency—the frequency of measurement that clearly identifies the level of service being experienced by the customer in relationship to Ultimate Service. The frequency of measure is not too great as to impose on the customer and not too low as to not clearly identify the service experience level.

Ultimate Service—is the highest possible service to the customer (either internal or external). Achieved when everyone is in the Pull of their internal and external customers.

Ultimate Service Flow—the best possible service is flowing through the people in the organization to the external customer.

Undefined Pull (weak Pull)—at least 1 of the Four Pull Questions is not answered or does not have agreement between supplier and customer.

Wisdom—knowledge gained from the experience of Measures of Success on how something works. According to Jonah Salk, the source of wisdom lies in the measures.

Appendix D — Resources

On Purpose / Vision / Mission

The Art of Possibility, Zander, Rosamund Stone & Benjamin, Harvard Business school Press, 2000
Contains excellent ideas on vision development

The Fifth Discipline, Senge, Peter M., Currrency Doubleday, 1994
The Art & Practice of The Learning Organization

First Things First, Covey, Stephen R., Fireside, 1992
Provides You With a Compass. Because Where You're Headed is More Important Than How Fast You're Going

The Pursuit of Wow, Peters, Tom, Vintage Books, 1994
Ideas for out of the box vision

On Measures of Success / Values / Measurement

The Balanced Scorecard, Kaplan, Robert S. and Norton, David P. HBS Press, 1996
Translating Strategy into Action
Has excellent ideas for including non-financial measures in business performance measurements

The Six Sigma Revolution, Eckes, George, John Wiley, Inc., 2001
How General Electric and Others Turned Process Into Profits
Good resource for ideas for subjective and objective measurements on Ultimate Service

The Power of Alignment, Labovitz, George and Rosansky, Victor, John Wiley & Sons, 1997
Aligning measurement and strategy to customer service.
Diagnostics for alignment are presented.

The HR Scorecard, Becker, Huselin, Ulrich, HBS Press, 2001
Looking at using balanced scorecard from a human resource view. Has many ideas for non-financial measurements. Presents business case for linking people, strategy, and performance.

360 Degree Feedback, Edwards, Mark R. and Ewen, Ann J., AMACOM, 1996
The Powerful New Model for Employee Assessment & Performance Improvement
Contains excellent source for ideas on tying personal performance to the Service Flow Pull Structure.

The Wisdom of Teams, Katzenbach, Jon R. and Smith, Douglas K. HarperBusiness, 1994
Creating the High-Performance Organization
Good measures on being a team, vision / mission development, performance and accountability.

Best Practices In Customer Service, American Management Association, edited by Ron Zemke & John A. Woods, HRD Press, 1998
A good resource from dozens of customer service experts who explain and demonstrate how to implement the best practices available in measuring customer service.

The Research Methods Knowledge Base, by William Trochim, Ph.D., Cornell University, available as an online edition or paperback (www.atomicdog.com). This is a comprehensive text for undergraduate and graduate social science research courses.

A Dictionary of Units of Measurement, written by Russ Rowlett, Director, Center for Mathematics and Science Education, University of North Carolina at Chapel Hill. This is an online dictionary on metric units of measure available only at: www.unc.edu/~rowlett/units/index.html

The Oliver Wight ABCD Checklist for Operational Excellence, Fifth Edition, Wight, Oliver, Oliver Wight Publications, Inc., 2001
A great resource for measurements

On Flow Implementation

The Quantum Leap, Costanza, John R., John Costanza Institute of Technology, Inc., 1996
Demand Flow Technology & Business Strategy
Contains patented formulas for implementing product flow in manufacturing and explains flow based costing, customer demand based flow without the traditional scheduling approach.

Lean Thinking, Womack, James P. and Jones, Daniel T., Simon & Schuster, 1996
Banish Waste and Create Wealth in Your Corporation
Understanding how to implement flow in manufacturing and how to find and eliminate non-value added activities to produce lean business processes.

Toyota Production System, Monden, Yasuhiro, Engineering & Management Press, 1998
Has very detailed and technical tools for understanding and implementing flow manufacturing.

On Organizations, Structure, Growth and Change

Servant Leadership, Greenleaf, Robert K., Paulist Press, 2002
An excellent understanding of how the Boardroom and Executive leadership are the most powerful when service mindedness prevails.

The Transparent Leader, Baum, Herb, Harper Business, 2004
Provides examples of how true leaders bring integrity to the
organization through complete honesty, transparency, accessibility
and courage. Transparency is shown to be the foundation for trust,
growth and change as well as the foundation for a service minded
culture.

Adaptive Enterprise, Haeckel, Stephan H., HBS Press, 1999
This excellent easy to read book that presents many ideas and
theories that are aligned with Pull Thinking applied to business.

Whole-Scale Change, Dannemiller Tyson Associates, Berrett-Koehler
Publishers, Inc., 2000
An excellent resource for ideas and principles of systems thinking
that draws on the wisdom of the organization itself. A handbook is
also available.

Leadership and the New Science, Wheatley, Margaret J., Barrett-
Koehler Publishers, 1999
Excellent book on applying the new science of chaos to
organizations of all types as well as to our personal lives.

Good to Great, Collins, Jim, HarperCollins Publishers, Inc., 2001
Understanding how to develop shared passion and going beyond the
normal service environment in business. Many examples of what
makes companies great. The behavior and characteristics of the
Hedgehog is used as a useful metaphor for business strategy in the
Hedgehog concept.

The Fifth Discipline, Senge, Peter M., Currency Doubleday, 1994
The Art & Practice of The Learning Organization
Excellent resource for vision and mission development as well as
strategies that involve people in creating the Ultimate Service
environment discussed in Pull Thinking.

Principle-Centered Leadership, Covey, Stephen R., Fireside, 1992
Has a great philosophy for creating more meaningful relationships
and successes in the workplace.

Beyond Reengineering, Hammer, Michael, HarperBusiness, 1996
How the Process-Centered Organization is Changing Our Work
and Our Lives

The Goal, Goldratt, Eliyahu M., North River Press, 1984
Theory of Constraint tools to where to look to improve the flow of
service. A process for ongoing improvement

The Natural Laws of Business, Koch, Richard, Currency Doubleday,
2000
How to Harness the Power of Evolution, Physics, and Economics to
Achieve   Business Success
Applies the theories of Darwin, Einstein, and Newton to achieve
business success.
This book is very close to Pull Thinking.

Soaring With the Phoenix, Belasco, James A. & Stead, Jerre, Warner
Books, 1999
This is a great resource for vision development. Lessons for
individuals truly interested in tapping into their own potential.

Leadership and the New Science, Wheatley, Margaret J., Barrett-
Koehler Publishers, 1999
This book shows how the New Science of Chaos points to the future
of organizational development and leadership.

Competing for the Future, Gary Hamel and CK. Prahalad (1994)
Looks at competition in an environment aligned to service.

Improving Performance, Rummler, Geary A., and Brache, Alan P., Jossey-Bass, 1995
Contains many ideas for changing the business structure.

Good Service is Good Business, Devry, Catherine, Career Press, 2001
Contains simple strategies for improving customer service and the economics of it. An easy read.

Raving Fans, Blanchard, Ken and Bowles, Sheldon, William Morrow and Company, Inc.1993
A common sense approach to customer service both internal and external

Who Moved My Cheese, Spencer Johnson, M.D. (1998)
An Amazing Way to Deal with Change in Your Work and in Your Life

Flight of the Buffalo, Belasco, James A., Warner Books, 1993
Soaring to Excellence, Learning to Let Employees Lead.
This is an excellent book on empowering people.

Thriving on Chaos, Peters, Tom, Perennial Library, 1988
Handbook for a Management Revolution

The Agenda, Hammer, Michael, Crown Business, 2001
Running Your Business For Your Customers

The Service Profit Chain, Heskett, Sasser, Schlesinger, The Free Press, 1997
There are many case studies showing businesses linking employee loyalty to service and profit.

Improving Performance, Gary A. Rummler and Alan P. Brache (1995)
How to Manage the White Space on the Organization Chart
A Practical Guide for Managing Organizations, Processes, and Jobs

On Being a Team, Choosing Team Members, Making Personal Choices

The Wisdom of Teams, Katzenbach, Jon R. and Smith, Douglas K.
HarperBusiness, 1994
Creating the High-Performance Organization. Good measures on being a team, vision / mission development, performance and accountability.

The Work of Teams, Katzenbach, Jon R., HBS Press, 1998
A collection of essays from Harvard Business Review articles

The Energetic Manager, Pryor, Fred, Prentice Hall, 1987
About growing cooperation, creativity and energizing everyone in the organization

Don't Waste Your Talent, McDonald, Bob, Ph.D., Longstreet Press, Inc., 2000
Presents eight critical steps to discover what you do best.

On Teams, Archer, Ron, McGraw-Hill, 1996
Great tools and measures for developing teams. Easy and fun to read.

Right Person — Right Job, Guess or Know, Russell, Chuck, Chuck Russell, 1996
Understanding people, their performance and the legal environment.

On Identity and Management

Maslow On Management, Maslow, Abraham H., John Wiley & Sons, Inc., 1998
Discussing businesss and management in relation to human needs and the concept of self-actualization and empowerment.

On Acknowledgement and Rewards

1001 Ways to Reward Employees, Nelson, Bob, Workman Publications, 1994

1001 Ways to Energize Employees, Nelson, Bob, Workman Publications, 1997

Punished by Rewards, Kohn, Alfie, Houghton Mifflin Company, 1993
What not to do. How money does not work.

Video

Passion for Customers, Peters, Tom, Video Publishing House, Inc. 1987
67 minutes, comes with workbook
5 case studies presented of business going for Ultimate Service flow and chronicled by Tom Peters.

Esoteric Reading (Going Beyond Business)

The Fourth Way, Ouspensky, P.D., Vintage Books, 1956
Contains ideas taught by the late P.D. Ouspensky, a Russian author, since 1921. This work is a result of studies by students of his work from about 10,000 pages of transcripts now in the Archives & Manuscripts Department of Yale University Library. A fourth way

of thinking (similar to Pull Thinking) discussed in terms of universal ideas and principles applied to life in general.

Flow, The Psychology of Optimal Experience, Csikszentmihalyi, Mihaly, Harper & Row, 1990
In Pull Thinking, the "Optimal Experience" occurs when there is Ultimate Service Resonance. This book verifies the importance of understanding flow.

Chaos: Making a New Science, Gleick, James, Penguin Books, 1987
How science is rethinking how they view the universe. It is about looking at measurement differently in order to see order in chaos that could not be identified before.

Strategy of the Dolphin, Lynch, Dudley, & Kordis, Paul, Fawcett Columbine Book, 1988
Seeing business strategies in terms of thinking from a flow perspective.

Acknowledgements

A special note of appreciation to:

J. Archer, my wife and partner for her untiring support and the many countless hours spent in editing and development;

Jeff Lebow, Vice President Business Development, Alignment at Work, LLC, for hard work, networking, support, editing, and writing assistance;

John Adcox, for book design, writing assistance, comprehensive editing;

Mary Embree, for writing assistance and comprehensive editing;

Sandra Tieman, for the cover design

Sharon Box, Principal of Out of the Box Creative, for the three dimensional color artwork and diagrams.

Gratitude and appreciation to these friends and colleagues who have contributed in many ways: Paul Aldo, Ken Boggs, Scott Beaver, Donna Calvert, Kathie Dannemiller, Stephan Haeckel, Liisa Hardaloupas, Charles Hoff, Kevin Howarth, Sheri Kling, Jeff Kazanow, Peter Korman, Ed Laake, Kim Leonard, Arthur Lerner, Robert Lowe, Thom Milkovic, Vee Nelson, Loren Platzman, Randy Randolph, Al Schaaf, Kathy Shirley, Gus Whalen, and Mike Wittenstein.